TABLE OF CONTENTS

FOREWORD

I have known Mike Boissonneault for nearly forty years. When he approached me regarding this book proposal, I could think of no one better suited or qualified to tackle the subject matter. He was on the ground breaking floor of a then little known startup company called ESPN (and later their parent Walt Disney Company) where he served for 35 years as an integral part of various aspects of their immense success, most notably in their Human Resources department. To know Mike is to immediately feel valued, listened to and ultimately motivated. What wonderful principles to be able to instill in others! Integrity, as well, is not something he hopes or wishes for, rather he insists upon it. He embodies it and it is no small wonder he has experienced the success he has because of it.

Having spent nearly twenty years as a "first and second tier manager" within the retail industry myself, as well as almost another fifteen years as public high school English teacher, I can attest to the value of harnessing and employing a strong set of "soft management" skills. But how does one actually attain such skills? Typically by being "thrown into the fire" as a result of a new job, or more accurately, a job promotion. Or perhaps you are enterprising enough to be embarking upon a new business startup yourself. How wish I had then, the tools and insight that you will now soon possess! With the book you are about to read, Mike imparts an understandable, structured approach to such effective know-how and leadership.

"Great!" You say. But how can you hone these skills and attributes in yourself as a manager, as well as in your workforce? You're already too busy, drained, overworked, etc. Your dilemma is about to be solved. With his book Mike conveys a truly systematic, organized offering. An indomitable self-starter, he has already done the hard part(s)! As you read the following pages it will become abundantly clear that diplomacy, advocacy, training, diversity, teamwork and trust are some of the most crucial components of Mike's game plan. Perhaps you are thinking, "Okay, but these are buzz words and rhetoric that I've heard before." And I am sure that you have! However, have you actually seen them come to *successful* fruition in your business or workplace? Something tells me that you have not or you would not still be searching for them. Clearly "Something's Missing." Well, my friend, the good news is that you have found it!

For a moment, let us consider just some of many the proposals Mike has effectively contributed towards and fostered, among them ESPN employer branding, as well as the Disney "Heroes Work Here" program (a concept, worth noting, that Mike actively helped bring to culmination). To use a sports analogy that Mike would appreciate (although he is far too humble to accept the following well-earned moniker): Mike Boissonneault is a Major Leaguer. He is the Big Time. *His leadership and expertise have resulted in ongoing legacies that are helping to change peoples' lives.* Again, with over 35 years of institutional knowledge--much of which he has helped to *create*—he has accomplished such outcomes with a set of "Soft Skills and Leadership" clearly worth noting!

While this book offers a wealth of support and wisdom for all who read it, those individuals in that transformative stage (whether it be via a job promotion or a new business startup) will surely find the greatest value from Mike's wisdom and experience. Use it! Throughout his book he will share valuable educational anecdotes and scenarios. As I stated previously: Mike has *already done* the hard part and essentially is now laying the groundwork for you. And what time consuming, challenging, and rewarding groundwork he has accomplished. And now you can as well with so much less worry.

As you read *Soft Skills & Leadership - HR Insight for Managers*, Mike notes that building "trust in the process" is paramount. And here he is, giving you that process. For example, as he discusses topics such as the difference between learning and training, the reader begins to understand how such seemingly small strategic thought shifts have large outcomes. Again, to use a sports analogy (you're welcome Mike!) consider how perhaps a batting or pitching coach can help correct a player in a slump. Mike Boissonneault is your coach and he is at your service.

Read the following pages. Use the tools and advice that is given here. You will not be disappointed. You value your time and Mike understands that. His book is written in an engaging, clear and effective manner. Virtually nowhere will you scratch your head wondering "What does he mean by that?" Rather you will say, "Yes! Finally! Now I am ready." Ready and armed with a better understanding of exactly what "soft skills" actually are. Excited to hone the ones that you may already possess. And most importantly, eager to employ many new ones found here that will ensure your future success.

Like a great coach, Mike Boissonneault throughout his business and HR career has listened, innovated, implemented and most importantly experienced success. Many times over. And now you will too. The following pages will serve you well in any and all your management and HR endeavors. Welcome to the Big Leagues!

Angela Dihlman Deslauriers

ABOUT THE AUTHOR

Mike Boissonneault is an experienced management and leadership consultant. He spent 35 years at ESPN and The Walt Disney Co., where he teamed with pioneers who forged innovative ways to produce sporting events. Subsequently, Mike contributed to transformative changes in Human Resources and specifically in Talent Acquisition and College Internships. He was a charter member of ESPN's first Diversity Task Force and was innovative in Training and Organizational Development while in Operations.

Mike is Founder and CEO of Rewirement Media, Inc., a cross platform web and television ecosystem that targets 50 year and older adults with a variety of consumable pods of entertainment, information and relevant content to lead active, healthy and inspired lives. RewirementMedia.com is the digital companion to what he calls *Generation Prime*, who today pursue life interests and changes across a new horizon and not ready for a traditional retirement existence. Rewirement Media, Inc. offers compelling content on Rewire TV and online publishing in sectors such as Health, Wealth, Insurance, Literature, Franchising, Fitness, Nutrition, Technology, Hobbies, DIY, Travel, Family Dynamics and Senior Living. Mike is teaming with influencers from these various industries to provide fresh and aspirational support to those 50 and older on the benefits of aging.

He is a published contributor and adviser on the University of New Haven's MS Sport Management board. Mike continues to teach and speak at businesses and universities regarding leadership. He is a proud SHRM member and outspoken proponent of core Human Resources roles.

PREFACE

How Did I Get Here?

I have been quite fortunate in my career. I began working in local media before I graduated from college and that experience helped so much in defining how I would approach work, treat others and set standards for personal performance. I worked independently in Radio and College Sports Writing and spent 17 of the coolest months of my life working at an NBC affiliate nearby. Clearly the pay was not a motivating factor in working there. Excitement and adrenaline ruled when a small business allowed me to run as fast as I could. It worked and was inspiring as well as motivating to me.

The break of a lifetime was being an early recruit at ESPN. They founded it one town away from me. I didn't realize I was joining true media pioneers and soon be on the cusp of popular cultural changes. Throughout my early years there, I fought for ethical and compliant decisions and assignments. I wanted so much to see our small company grow and succeed and we all had enormous pride in our work and ourselves and we formed an indomitable team. We were small in numbers and going in dozens of directions. We worked together, across divisions and experiences. We pursued excellence and tolerated great effort and allowed a few mistakes. We wore several hats and buoyed each other. The culture was taking effect. All for one.

What I learned most of all, was the importance of stepping back at times and taking a hard look at who we were and where we thought we were headed. It's difficult to do that when you're so busy, your head is down and you're clearly crushing it in the public eye, cultivating the consumer connection and the fans are recurring. When I started to look more closely at the makeup, how we were set at the foundation and at the top, I found some flaws. We needed depth and diversity. I learned from my sports background that eventually skills diminish, people leave and the next generation needs to be conditioned to take over. Even in a division as large as our Operations was growing towards, we needed to ensure future stability.

Our "Personnel" group was undergoing a transformational change to "Human Resources". They were on-site and somewhat small for the type and scope of business we were cultivating. As managers, some of us took the reins and made sure our divisions stayed on track, in hiring, performance managing, training and development, etc. It was time to roll up the sleeves and help.

Due mostly to my reputation as someone not afraid to knock on doors outside my division, such as Sales, Marketing and Programming, I was thought of as a "go to" person. I created opportunities for the Operations teams to be in on early decision making and strategic planning.

I built up a good reputation as a team player by the time I helped HR in their expansion years. I was diplomatically outspoken and therefore called often by the HR team to step in and help when new programs were upcoming. I helped to train entry levels through executives on a number of programs, systems and applications of good, centralized HR. I felt that I was a bridge and not afraid to support either or both sides on project plans and management. They brought in new Business Partners and

Diversity leaders. They brought in Learning and Development specialists and world class Staffing (soon to be Talent Acquisition) leaders. Each time, I was brought into meet & greets and help usher them into the company. It was more than exhilarating, it was intoxicating. I felt respected and was humbled to help out. It is with this background that I transferred from an executive role in Production Operations to one in Human Resources. Not quite a fish out of water, but I learned that a front row seat in HR for ESPN and ultimately The Walt Disney Company, was a chance of a lifetime.

Therefore, when I transitioned into the HR world officially, no one blinked an eye. Many thought I was already there. We were transformative in all HR areas. I talked regularly to everyone in the department and met frequently with my Disney counterparts as well. This gave me more insight and education than I could have ever found externally. I am forever grateful for that stretch of my career.

The four years in Human Resources flew by and the benefits included helping to make changes in employer branding, creating a workforce operations team in talent acquisition, helping with on boarding, partnering with diversity, delving into compensation studies and contributing to the learning team on a number of projects. To think that my career started as a chance to go into sports production and studio operations at a small startup called ESPN and here I was making decisions and contributing to the future plans for this incredible global brand. I played a founding part of the inception for the Heroes Work Here program at Disney, acclimating military veterans to civilian life and job searching. Through 2017, Heroes Work Here has influenced nearly 25,000 hires in Disney and other companies who came through the program. So worthwhile.

I retired at a very young age and started a consulting company, focusing on management skills and leadership. My HR background is clearly a source of pride and gratitude. As I remember the teams, the consultants, organizations, the workforce and all those who have had influence on me over the years, my values and beliefs have clearly been shaped by dozens of people. If this path could happen to me, it can certainly be repeated for you in other industries. Keep your horizon wide and take risks on yourself to learn horizontally as I refer to it. Learning from the left or right flank will help you better comprehend how your company churns.

Now, to this book. I am very supportive of HR as well as business management. I know in many situations and environments there could be better working relationships or environments. My goal is that you read this as a business manager and have a new perspective on the other side. I am not the expert on all things HR, but have a true belief and personal conviction for the support and integrity that good business leadership brings. HR by nature is a well-educated and compliant community and through this book I hope to offer insight to what they do for you and provoke your interest in HR roles and responsibilities as your personal training tool.

Throughout this publication, I'll call the staff the workforce, refer to the environment of the business as the workplace and identify the external world as both the marketplace and/or the competition. I use the term "we" throughout the book because of the emphasis many people and organizations have personally had on me through the years. There are many external and internal factors that have shaped my way of thinking and dealing with workforce, workplace and marketplace with respect to the business at hand. I've had the great opportunity to work with top influencers, consultants and world leading HR organizations as well as colleagues and associates who were ground breaking in thought and action. I'll start a list at the end of Chapter 10. This is a partial, but very important recognition of the influencers on my HR background.

I feel that my vision and disposition regarding the advocacy of and acceptance for HR is now somewhat unique as I learn from everyone I associate with. Therefore, aside from a couple dictionary definitions, no internet or outside research was used directly and I stand by this work as an outpouring of my staunch regard for the integrity of a better HR and Business Unit relationship.

Human Resources grew out of the aforementioned Personnel. It once was where you filled out job applications, got your company ID, doled out discipline, picked up your paycheck, signed up for benefits and likely sought personal assistance. Fast forward through the past 20 years and in fact, so much of today's Human Resources support is targeted directly to protecting the business, regarding decisions that need to be compliant and legal, that the term "Human" may not be as complete as it was intended to be. My contention is that the term Human Resources should be replaced simply by Advocacy. It's a softer term, not rooted in any historical connotation, and completely supportive of both the workforce and the business.

INTRODUCTION

An Open Letter to Managers

This book is designed to give Business Managers and aspiring Human Resources professionals a solid foundation and understanding of the many disciplines that encompass workforce management and business advocacy. My intent is to write it as an open letter to managers in any industry and all types of business. My experiences include managing in large teams and always striving for ethical and upstanding practices. This comprehensive array is quite contemporary. The best practices of current Human Resources and Workforce Management process and protocols will be covered, discussed, debated and absorbed through this book. I wrote it in the words and terms that business leaders and managers can understand and correlate to HR terms for balance. It's a conversation from me to you, an open letter about what I hope to impart.

I'll cover a wide breadth of subject material ranging from Organizational Development (Business Design) through Human Capital support (e.g. Talent Acquisition, Compensation, Learning, Diversity, Employee Relations) and cover areas of technological data management (e.g. Data and Analytics). Important areas of focus will include the roles of the Human Resources Generalist/Business Partner (Business Advocacy) and a discerning correlation between roles in Management and Leadership. My goal is to break down the HR disciplines into business language and general terms. This should allow you to absorb the content and self-direct your continuing learning. My mission is to make you more aware of HR roles and more valuable as a manager.

This book will take a slight diversion on the traditional path for learning Human Resources disciplines. HR is doing well in the hands of the *Society for Human Resource Management*, (SHRM) which leads in all the areas of thought leadership, training and certification in each of the HR fields. I am a proud member of SHRM, which is the leading HR organization with more than 285,000 members across the globe. https://www.shrm. org/ SHRM stays relevant and offers many opportunities to stay in touch with all the soft "people" skills and business support roles. The SHRM courses and conferences are expensive to participate in, and one is typically expected to be a practicing HR professional to join SHRM and take advantage of their benefits. You can get a good taste of the HR specialties by reading the book and continuing to practice soft skill management.

This book is intended to completely advocate on behalf of the skills involved in HR, but done so in business language and as common to the actual business lexicon rather than legal or HR terminology. It's also not my intention to shut out HR to business managers, but to create a valuable alternative, based on businesses and their critical needs. Many small, medium or larger size businesses cannot afford a full time or retained HR division and must find ways to solve these skills gaps where they can, to survive. In other businesses, introducing new managers to the HR disciplines is a way of building soft skills and trust in the process. Managers will be more valuable simply by learning, understanding and incorporating some of the accredited HR skill set.

Any new manager, with this information on various HR disciplines, can become more valuable and their role might offer more satisfaction and organization than before. It's time for first and second tier managers to have this institutional knowledge of how business, and theirs specifically, works. Armed with this knowledge, new managers can self-direct their continued growth through the myriad of information available every day from thought leaders, organizations, consultants and reference material that is, in most cases, free to consume. Something's missing if managers don't take advantage of it.

CHAPTER 1

Something's Missing

B usiness leaders are faced with many tasks in their daily routines. Owning or running a company, a division, a business unit or even leading a small team of employees has built in expectations. Managers are accountable for most everything that happens "on their watch".

America has an endless number of small companies and major corporations. No matter the size of the operation, people manage people. The life cycle of an employee is as significant a road map as the production supply chain for any product manufactured. It is imperative to have fair and equitable laws governing each stage of that process and evolution. Employment, by its very nature, drives personal and community growth on every level. Without rules and organization, businesses fail and the economy suffers. Something's missing.

An obvious path to answer the question of "What's missing?" would be to steer new managers towards Human Resources disciplines and training. This book will provoke thought and offer an array of information on creating, sustaining and transforming businesses. This is the start of the bridge building between any business management team and HR doctrines.

Organizational development and individual growth are areas of focus and deep discussion. Much of the typical design of companies are influenced by their specific industries and future business plans. We will delve into those areas to open dialogue and point to the currently available resources to back up the various schemes. Expanding the minds of business professionals to think broadly and act compliantly is a driver for the book. Human Resources professionals or programs can assist you.

Systems and processes change often and are greatly influenced by technology. We will focus on the theoretical practices and offer solutions and endorsements of some of the best business or human capital protocols and suggest applications available to support the various business and workforce management needs.

The workforce of the future is an important factor in any current business planning. Learning how to stay relevant and garnering the trust of the workforce is a paramount goal for Workforce Management. Another key derivative of the book can be incorporating a peripheral approach to understanding the expectations of the workforce, where a business fits into the supply chain of any given company or industry and ultimately how to leverage immediate and on-demand resources and/or trade organizations.

We anticipate that our readers will cross several demographics. Some will be attracted directly out of the school of business who may look to Human Resources as a target market for jobs. Others will be transitioning professionals who would like to either go into a management trek or an HR discipline. Still others, possibly the largest demographic, would be first and second tier (early) managers at companies big and small who need refresher courses and/or training in what we consider soft skills and Workforce

industry or company. You, as manager, must understand more of the company business plans and organization and therefore have a starting point for yourself and anyone reporting to you. Your company should have a template or data bank to enter your information to and memorialize the exercise annually. Otherwise, you should save documents and notes through the year for review.

Start with the job descriptions of your workforce. Are they up to date and you all have an understanding of expectations? If so, look at the daily workflow, the seasonal changes, the different opportunities through the calendar. Are the right people positioned to find basic success? If so, move on to the individuals. How are they set up in their current roles? Do their skills match your expectations for them and are they in a position you both can relate to the company organizational design? If so, move on. What is their role by specialty (e.g. Administration, Finance, IT, Sales, etc.). Are they progressing in that regard? Are they marketable in their skills and aspirations? If so, carve out some opportunities to build projects or goals for them individually to take advantage of skills and role to exceed the normal expectations of you performance year. Set up milestones and benchmarks. Set up touch point to review and adjust as you go.

Think of the year as twelve iterations on a project management plan and you are setting schedules for updates and status checks. Each of you should discuss current situations, conditions and assessment. What is the goal each period (week, month, quarter, year)? Collaborate and document the conversations. Ask for feedback from others who may be intervening or supervising in their routine assignments or project partnerships. Now you have data to provide a status report, looking back for review and ahead for new horizons to cross. This is fundamental managing.

How much time managers spend in the office will surely be scrutinized by the workforce, who feel they are too often disconnected with their managers. By contrast, how much time they spend "on the floor" may be questioned by their senior leadership who may feel they are too close to the staff. There are other factors to put into the balance equation. It seems like the newest managers have the least amount of autonomy when it comes to preferred shifts, assignments and other amenities of the position. The chance to grow a bit and spread the wings has often been replaced with harder deadlines, taking work home and odd times to work. Perhaps the promotion or opportunity to manage came with an exempt pay status. Somewhere in the meaning of the term "exempt" is the unwritten rule of being available whenever and wherever necessary and not punching a clock. Freedom is replaced with too much work and not enough time to complete tasks, let alone an opportunity to grow. Something's missing.

Workforce Needs Strong Managers

The workforce is generally "on the floor", operating, selling, completing tasks on a routine and often seasonal basis. Predicted by calendars, clocks and weather at times, the workforce knows what needs to be done, how long it takes and what effort will work best. In managing or leading, you will soon find out that those hard skills are in your background and the new people skills take some getting used to. Whether an athlete or a furniture sales person, the workforce is a specialized breed, honed by years of repetition and competition pushing them to do a better job. Authority is still close by during crunch time, but in the background, managers and leaders earn their stripes by planning strategically and executing, often through their teams, to beat the competition and satisfy those buying the product or service as well as those who own it or are invested in it.

The higher one rises as an individual contributor, the more they become specialists and in demand. Most individuals can still close the door and go home at the end of the day and find a work/life balance. If they need to stay longer or due to special circumstances, they are usually beneficiaries of extra compensation. The managerial ranks don't always enjoy that same allowance, many are caught in the fray, having to report or follow up on good and bad situations, and that is part of the job of managing. The early years in the role can be the most difficult, the transition, the communication, the true expectations and the changes in habits all contributing. Was all of this covered in the interview? A very common thought among early managers is simply that something's missing. Be careful what you ask for.

Many staff who have been below the line of management may not have the opportunity to train or try out for the role ahead of time and it makes a difficult situation when an opening is posted and leadership must consider, whether (or not) to include newbies. These may be loyal, hard-working and very successful, impactful and influential team leaders as individuals, but what happens when they cross over and become the boss? How quickly can they acclimate to the new responsibilities and how will they adapt to the changes associated with peers, subordinates and executives? How much time and what resources will it take for them to come up to speed when a company could easily look outside for a seasoned or more experienced manager?

An essential competency that is not easily trained for is communication. In every aspect of human interaction, a manager is measured by how they receive, dispense, report and/or negotiate information. Managers should speak not only on behalf of their company leaders but as the company itself. By contrast, a staff employee is generally considered as a contributor to the news and observation, not held to a standard that would be part of a division's management team. Normal conversation changes when managers enter a room or area where others congregate for social or other interaction. It's part of human nature not to reveal everything in front of the boss. Until someone lives in that role it's hard to know the feeling, especially the emotional detachment from your workforce. Something's missing in the transition plan. How has diplomacy become so much of a manager's tool kit?

Filling the role of manager could involve some tangled relationships. Do you promote from within or go outside? The leadership or hiring team must weigh the difference between someone who knows the business well and is gearing to be a manager versus an (external) experienced professional who must learn the specific business and gain the confidence and acceptance of the inherited workforce. How adept is the leadership and hiring team at assessing these requirements? In this book, we'll cover how to organize and bring true structure to the recruitment and interview process. In that sense, we'll explain how to use a non-biased and equitable approach to filling the roster, especially when it comes to filling coveted roles in management.

There is a condition that was originally brought to light in 1969 called the *Peter Principle*, originated by Laurence J Peter. He contended that "the selection of a candidate for a position is based on performance in their current role rather than on abilities relevant to the intended role." https:// en.wikipedia.org/wiki/Peter_principle This is an institutional flaw in some companies and industries. Many of these types of failures in hiring or promoting can result in poor management, lower productivity and morale. The mistake can often have grave financial consequences and cost much more to repair rather than replace.

answers are critical to building a foundation and a successful business plan. Products and services are often part of a collaborative effort to get to the market. There are inherent obstacles in any supply chain, including delays and unforeseen emergencies. How the company deals with countering these obstacles will be a measurable and necessary step in ensuring success. Businesses should continually assess and repair the supply channels to keep products and services flowing to the marketplace on timed releases. There are some great programs that teach a continual and effective monitoring and measuring of business.

It should be noted that not all roles in a company are directly tied to the flow of products and services and what the company delivers as its core output. However they all have at least an indirect impact on work flow. For example, the finance groups analyze spend and budget forecasts, oversee the general ledger, balancing capital, operating expense and receivables, in addition to analyzing and allocating funds throughout the business. This is a standard for most businesses, scaled as necessary. They may not be on the supply chain to get products and services out to the market, but certainly key staff ensuring the reliability of funds and reports. Many divisions of a company do specific and specialized work, which aggregated, will help build the entire business. There are core roles that every company need to consider when laying out the organizational design, including sales, finance, marketing, administration, etc. These all are specialized roles, some with certification, such as accounting or HR, that should be considered when deciding how much depth to add internally to your staff or external outsourcing to complete the business design.

As an early manager, you should have a broad understanding of some of the questions posed. In Business Design, it's as important to understand the layout of jobs and responsibilities as much as the flow of information and distribution of products and/or services. Managers should equip themselves with this basic type of information and listen to the workforce when they speak up about anything that may impede or improve that flow. Listening is a critical competency of managers and doesn't automatically mean you make changes, it just means that you collect as much information and data as necessary when making decisions. Small decisions require less detail and swifter action. For example, where to place a work bench or a storage cabinet certainly doesn't require as much research, study and collaboration as implementing new technologies or staffing. Design and Architecture require a constant and consistent analysis and review.

Workflow also considers how other centralized areas, such as finance or marketing, work. Each has a hierarchal structure where the entry level roles work more administratively or tactically, and the more advanced or managerial roles have responsibility to provide solutions, reports and deliverables on behalf of the division. Also, it's worth noting that in many cases of designing a business, these roles are what's known as transferable and with a little institutional knowledge, can be shared amongst disparate industries. Bottom line, many of these roles can be outsourced, contracted or otherwise economically implemented and those decisions are part of business design. In many cases, the larger a company becomes, the more it relies on specialization in certain niche, essential areas to compete in. That helps define what industry you perform in.

Information technology is an important facet of business. Information about employees, business deals, policies and procedures, payroll, performance management, etc., are all essential elements to gather and contain discreetly. IT covers everyone and everything in business, from rights and permissions to employee personal data. The IT networking franchise is as important as sales and services divisions. How does IT work in your business structure?

Building a Business

An organizational (org) chart is a key representation of a company, no matter the size. It is a depiction of the charter of a company. Each box (role) represents responsibility, growth and development, financial oversight and certain performance expectations. Several divisions of the company view the org chart from different points of view. Human Resources may view it for organizational structure, management work flow and pay scale. The IT group may see this as which levels or roles gain more access to systems and information and the finance team will enforce parameters on systems access, spending, expensing and financial approvals. Good organizational design allows for interactive and flexible role interpretation.

When designing an org chart, think of the terms *roster* (all names), *real estate* (area of responsibility) and *ranking* (title). Each employee should be accounted for on the chart once. Start at the top of the company and draw the "pyramid" which depicts a shape that represents the responsibility each owns or shares. The most economically efficient example would be to design more staff level and less management, which allows production line effectiveness for the least amount of management or executives necessary to be successful. That's cost effective.

Classifying Roles

The roles and areas of responsibility inside the company are important to understand and are identified by their titles. Proper titles allow a leader to lay out a chain of command. If done correctly, areas of growth are identified and the reporting structure is evident. Entry level and advanced level should be clearly delineated. The growth of a role can be attributed to a job family, where the roles increase in both skills and responsibilities as they go up towards more advanced levels. The titles are important to the individual and the marketplace will confirm whether compensation is fair and equitable. It's important to know why roles have certain value or salary. There are many factors that go into the value of a job and will be covered in more detail in the next chapter. This further demonstrates the interdependency of the HR roles. For now, we can discuss some basic criteria.

The classification of a role is an official status and affects benefits and other entitlements. This is also an important piece of business design. For example, a full-time employee may have certain rights not offered to a contract or part time employee. The hierarchal structure simply means that the areas of responsibility fit the role and expertise of the management and that the roles reporting directly or indirectly to them fit some defensible criteria as well. This is covered more extensively in the compensation roles as part of data and market analysis.

So, how are the roles defined? Managers should understand those roles below their line and within their organization. They need to be able to speak to the responsibilities, the work expectations and any other relevant criteria that would be important to recruiting on the role or managing the people who perform in them. Building a business from the foundation up through management is a challenge of design. Do the jobs escalate correctly and do the responsibilities increase proportionately? Can the managers educate, evaluate and manage the ones they supervise or do they share performance management duties with other leaders? How is performance management tied to the org chart? Does the foundation support the C-Suite?

Verticals and horizontals comprise an org chart, especially in matrix organizations. Headers depict the "real estate", divisional or other terminology for the responsibility they share or oversee. The vertical roles must graduate from bottom to top in "like positions", showing growth potential by titles. These collectively become the "job families". As an exercise, build out your division or business unit as an org chart and assess whether, or not, the roles and responsibilities increase as you go from foundation to management. There may be horizontal (centralized) assignments, for example HR or Finance roles, which support all the divisions. It's a great presentation to show how the organization's efficient setup helps cover necessary business needs and all employees would be more valuable if they understood the basics of this structure.

Balancing Responsibilities

Some important details a manager needs to understand include the responsibilities and requirements associated with the roles and people that report to them. Are the responsibilities common to their industry or are they uniquely attributed to your company? This helps to figure out the complexity of the role and determine if it becomes too tied specifically to the company and not to the actual role. There can be a lot of overhead associated with getting too unique as specialization usually aligns with extra compensation. This could lead to an adverse manager/subordinate relationship and undue stress. In some cases, it's worth the uniquely structured roles as a retention strategy, but in many cases, will not end up well. We won't go too deep on this point, as the recruitment and talent acquisition teams should help carve out roles and responsibilities based on market strengths and talent pools. How many total staff in those positions that you'll need is based upon many factors, such as the volume of your business, schedule of operations, nature of role (entry level or minimum wage/high turnover), required supervision, etc. Once the responsibilities are thought through and balanced amongst the team and business, the organizational chart will become a very valuable tool.

The more advanced a business, the more the org chart takes on different meanings based on the point of view. Financial roles and permissions can be linked to an org chart, by individual role, by a grade level, by a base salary or a job description. Those roles could include expense allowances as well as any approval rights, or how much money one may be accountable for in a retail role, for example. The higher the role, the more valuable in terms of finance can be expected. Similarly, performance management roles can be aligned to the chart. Perhaps at the staff level, the expectations of knowledge to perform the role, skills to be offered as a trainer and what skills or responsibilities are necessary to advance would be tied in. This is a typical application of adhering performance management to the org chart. Add in the subordinate to supervisor or manager relationships and it's easy to depict the performance evaluation teams.

Business Flow

A comprehensive understanding of your business plan is a recipe for success. There are simple as well as complex facts and procedures. Among them include the business location. Is there a home office with multiple spaces, buildings, offices, etc.? Are there multiple locations (e.g. retail, banking, fast food, etc.) that work off centralized or franchise plans? Knowing where business is conducted is important as many transactions can occur in the virtual world. There are many reasons for specifically locating business, such as tax and zoning restrictions. Where does your employee base go to work and where do your consumers find solutions? As business climate changes, business may grow or possibly face contraction.

Part of business planning deals with the various work flows. To understand how business flows, start by researching how your products are made, who is responsible (and how) to get materials for the processes, how you reach your customers, deadlines, etc. Today in the software world, applications, WiFi and other factors have an important place in business flow. Who do you compete with and will that factor in your own business formulas? How are your processes governed? Do you know of any laws, regulations or variances that may restrict or improve your productivity? In your industry, are you competing for talent or services? Business planning affirms and often confirms your business flow, projects expense and revenue generation accurately and predicts how and when success may be measured. Business planning is a good opportunity to look at your company as it relates to the specific industry or industries that it aligns to.

Vendor Management

It's very important to understand best practices concerning vendor management. Communication is critical to keeping aware of each other's expectations. There are plenty of support books and blogs concerning proper vendor management and recommendation is to convey this as business critical. There may have been many Service Level Agreements (SLAs), for example, in a vendor relationship. Workflow and expectations of products, services and deliveries are negotiated as well as any shared or split responsibilities. Each of these terms are critical to success and financial arrangements. Good communication protocols will ensure transparent understanding and enduring partnerships.

Other areas that require your focus, depending on the size and flow include sales and marketing. Do you sell or lease your own space or service offerings? Are your sales in the form of products to consumers through third party retail or wholesale vendors? Knowing where your results are will be key indicators in measuring success. What are your timelines for deliverables and how do you schedule your normal operations? Is your business dependent on individual sales orders or corporate accounts with recurring volume? How do you market your business and to whom? Many questions and we are only scratching the surface of understanding how your business flows. Having an ongoing dialogue with senior leaders will help all managers to feel more confident about their roles and responsibilities to overall business flow.

Brand Management and Change Management

Building a successful organization takes strategic planning and culture is also a key component. Creating and sustaining a brand that resonates with your customers, vendors and especially your staff should be a common goal. A good employee base starts with an organized mission and values statement that the company can stand by, live up to and align with vendors and consumers alike. The brand is your shield. It should be nurtured and protected by all who work in the organization. Craft a good mission statement and require that all employees understand it and embody it. We will assume your company is established and has a brand. It's a good practice for management to learn about the brand, it's message and how to protect it.

When your business changes, how are the components announced, enabled, enacted or implemented? How do your vendors and consumers get the information on changes? How do you make changes within your organization? Do you encourage all employees for input or only at the top? Is it different to make changes to policies and workflow versus changes to products and services? These are key components with respect to management styles and internal communications that fuel success. Good organizational structure will allow for efficient communication with respect to recommended changes and certain policies and announcements both internally and externally.

Managers should allow the staff to discuss conditions of work, something staff will be very partisan on, because the opportunity to input for change is important. In some businesses, this may not be the norm, so figure out the flow of information for your company and not be surprised later. It's also good to set expectations when you open the floor for discussions, as not all suggestions or complaints will enact change. And not all change ends up being popular, so temper the discussions and keep them open, honest and genuine. Don't ask for input if there is no chance at all of change, instead use the time to practice good change management techniques, something we won't go into much detail here but will advocate on behalf of. Change management is among the most sought after skills for leaders.

Leveraging Support

It's vitally important for managers to understand where their business sits within a specific industry. Setting some benchmarks to compare products, services, market presence, trends, etc., will provide managers a sense of where the company ranks and what might be worth exploring, to change, improve or sustain a status. How will a manager gain insight and confidence in acquiring knowledge and skills and applying the newfound learning?

Start with research. There are numerous companies, organizations and individual experts or practitioners who discuss and detail their best practices on line each day. Most individual roles in an organization can align their specialty job title to industry support or trade groups. Encourage and support the employees to seek out best practice or trades groups posted content so they can further develop skills, competencies and feel more valued overall. The more experienced and valued they feel, the more impact they will add to your company.

We encourage a lifelong commitment to learning and development. The specialty trades and industries have so many consultants, experts and practitioners willing to share and discuss issues, trends and solutions that most of the content is free to consume. Newsletters, blogs, opinion essays, etc. are available each day. The various social networks such as Facebook and LinkedIn all have platforms and forums devoted to specialty groups who share and debate best practices, opinions and new trends.

CHAPTER 3

Evaluating the Marketplace & Workplace

Employee data is a very necessary part of any company's files. For example, information regarding specifically who is either applying for or enrolled as an employee, along with such personal information as social security numbers, personal banking and insurance information, beneficiaries, salary, benefits and performance ratings must be recorded, stored and protected. This data is also, at any point in time, a snapshot to help determine the market value of a workforce. How does your company stack up against the industry? Data is a key indication of resource management and employee health. Analyzing and managing this data message becomes a critically sensitive and vital part of steering a business.

There are many ways and means to evaluating staff data and staying compliant with safeguarding data security. Human Resources professionals are trained and tasked with leading the efforts to collect, store, share and secure any employee data. That also includes setting value on roles and jobs, keeping companies competitive and aware of the emerging marketplace.

Shared Services

The Human Resources systems are generally off limits to those outside the division, unless there is no HR division and the manager or company front office may handle the compensation data and its processing. Many pieces of information are discreet, sensitive and legally protected. It's best practice to centralize the functions and repository of these information streams for access by those at the highest clearance and/or in HR roles. Management should understand what information should be kept under "lock and key" terms. The government mandates that employers protect data that includes information such as personal identifying classification, social security numbers and disciplinary reviews, for example. For companies that cannot afford to own and maintain secure systems, there are centralized resources and cloud storage available through reputable and highly regarded data companies.

Sharing the service and security is often a cost effective and efficient model. Buying a subscription and holding an experienced and forward thinking storage company accountable for the data input and reporting is a safe and smart way to do business. For the companies that can afford to own, innovate and maintain these systems, having the information on hand and available can be a great advantage in some cases.

Integrating the on-boarding and payroll systems with performance and benefits can create an efficient business model that can reap rewards when the employer is doing major changes, project management and annual reviews. It also allows for the company to efficiently forecast resources (both human and otherwise) as these systems can be interdependent and aligned.

Think of the possibilities of integrating some systems to help initiatives. For example, how would the benefits and payroll help forecasting new expansion of a business? Start with numbers of resources that might carry over, how much payroll would be, entitled time off, etc., and overall support from other centralized data points. Expanding on the manufacturing or supply chain may require new staffing, at various levels. Look at recent employee survey data to see of the current thought is that the company is staying relevant regarding technology. Is expansion being considered in an efficient way? Will it implement automation that may cause jobs to change drastically to be impacted? Consider performance management data to predict which of the current staff could be promoted or otherwise financially advancing and make better overall business decisions regarding expansion. This is a case for evaluating marketplace and workplace together.

It's essential to understand what type of information is protected and what specific data your company regards as discreet. Regarding research and analytics, there is one piece of information that is just as sensitive as any other, which is an employee's or consumer's answers to company surveys. Survey answers, while usually anonymous, can be revealing and only a few top company leaders can get that information when warranted. Still, survey data is a company resource for feedback, steering and threat analysis. There are many types of surveys that will ultimately collect and control personal data. Only reputable firms should be sourced to roll out surveys.

While analytics plays such an important part of business today, big data is very effective at predictive analysis. This is a part of business that helps make decisions regarding changes, merger and acquisition, etc. Determine what type of information is needed for the project and how that will come into the decision-making process.

Employee Data (HR) Systems

There are many systems, tools and vendors that comprise the Employee Data (HR) business. When researching which are the best to utilize, consider cost, effectiveness, reliability and security. There are very good consultants and vendors in this industry to help you evaluate and pick the right systems and tools for your specific application.

It's worth the time to research and compare the criteria for selecting what's right for your application of data management. Knowing your business well helps the decision making for the type of information you'll want to collect, retrieve, process and evaluate. Cost and intuition play an important part. You or your staff may have to use the system, so how intuitive is the processing, how easy is it to use and how can it be enhanced, updated and advanced for future applications or through company growth?

The correct system should have some interdependent role with other systems you employ, if possible. That will allow for merging data and reports without having to create additional interfaces to disseminate information while looking at overall performance or multiple data points. Same criteria should be used if you outsource some of your systems. If you outsource payroll, for example, how easy is it to get reports and combine with others that you have within your systems at the office? Is the data just as secure and is the interface effective?

Many of the systems that are controlled in these roles will house data and be summoned in certain legal proceedings or circumstances. Leaders who have access to this information should be reminded of their role in compliant recording and retrieving of any discreet data.

Compensation

Compensation is the term associated with balancing a monetary value to someone for work based upon, among other things, title, market comparisons and experience. Compensation has a few meanings, including one that is usually associated with law suits and injury settlements. For our course, we'll deal specifically with the money for work approach.

How valued are you and are your individual employees? How much data is analyzed and how many types of information or criteria is used to determine that number? Consider that there is a myriad of ways to determine value and for that summation, so we'll refer to the answer as "total rewards". The folks who work as compensation professionals will analyze all the data and come up with a grid for your business. If you don't outsource or hand off to HR Compensation, then consider all the factors and ensure they are equivalently and equitably distributed in your formula.

Compensation leaders also play a role in performance management solutions as they may own the information on salaries, bonus and annual merit awards. A business leader may work closely with a compensation partner to find the right balance of performance based awards, possibly through a separate annual budget that helps balance promotions as well as annual increases in pay. In companies with an internal or centralized compensation division this process is a formal way to provide checks and balances to both performance and the payroll budget.

Value added entitlements such as paid time off (PTO), insurance benefits, savings and investment plans, cash or stock incentives, pension plans, training platforms, other incidentals such as transportation subsidies, travel subsidies, potential discount programs, tuition reimbursement and other programs collectively add up to the total rewards figures.

HR Compensation professionals are experienced in analyzing the marketplace for salaries and roles compared to those in your business. This is an important step that works together with Business Design and Talent Acquisition on understanding the market and job values. Earlier, we briefly referred to job families. A job family should depict the graduation of positions and titles in a linear fashion. For example, consider job titles. Do they gradually go up in skills, such as a title with a number scheme (Role I – Role II – Role III) or name lineage (Associate – Manager – Director)? Are they all based upon industry or market averages, meaning roles and responsibilities are understood and based upon years of experience and abilities? Once established, they should be compared to the marketplace based on what specifically they do within your business, how growth is built in and where you are located. Some of the bigger markets are adjusted, as necessary, based upon cost of living and competition nearby. The reverse can be said for smaller markets.

Common terms such as "above the line" and "below the line" refer to where a role sits in management or on staff. In a job family, we create roles with requisite titles and the roles at the beginning of the string (perhaps at entry level) and those at the top of the individual contributor line (advanced or senior level) share a common core of skills and education. Many jobs (such as in technology or on a manufacturing line), may be easy to discern regarding the common core of skills and at each ascending level. Additionally, the expectations are to do more, with better results or accuracy and have decreasing dependence on direct supervision.

One can literally scale their job family with strong performance year after year and demonstrated improvements in skill. Add motivational criteria, such as early to work, helping to train others and suggesting new efficient solutions, and the responsibilities will naturally increase throughout

finesse and professionalism must rise to a level of trust, confidence and ultimately employee advocate at times.

Protocol - Handbook of Policies and Procedures

Successful company business should start with a well written and organized Employee Handbook. This is a defensible reference manual that both workforce and management can read and relate to. It should contain rules of professional conduct, scheduling, time off entitlements, general information and any known, standing policies that govern normal business operations. Additional information may contain benefits information, orientation or on boarding process and even protocol supporting separation and retirement. All information should be company specific. For those companies who are franchised or part of larger enterprises, a matrix of information is generally available.

Let's briefly examine what a handbook is and why it's such an important company statement. The handbook should state clearly some of the principals of the workplace and the workforce. It is compiled to set the standards of business operation, conduct and policy. It is defensible in investigations and legal proceedings. Its content includes many pieces of what is considered expected (i.e. normal) in work conditions and workplace. Some of the information must be generalized and other is quite specific. For example, hours of operation may be altered as necessary for business reasons while some of the employee benefits are strictly enforced.

The handbook is a public repository of information. Many of the parameters of business should be detailed to a point, without getting so specific that it hampers business practice from evolving. The specific information that enforces benefits and entitlements, most of which is tied specifically to milestones and hard facts or dates, can be spelled out and could include formulas for figuring out individual cases. On the other hand, conduct that can be reviewed and altered as warranted might include dress code and company observed holidays. There is a lot of information overall, so organizing and categorizing the handbook is critical. The handbook should not require daily or frequent changes, though there should be a consistent and official review as necessary, which will vary from company to company. Today, it should be filed virtually for immediate reference by all employees.

The employee lifecycle generally starts at orientation and runs through final separation, which may be voluntary, involuntary and/or retirement. Each of these general milestones has variances and in cases, obstacles and even some legal writ. The handbook will be a guide for most of the intermediary and long term employment state, and will require individual attention and legal intervention at some critical steps. On boarding is an initial phase for employees, which legally brings together employee and employer, and will be then "governed" in many cases, by the handbook. Managers have a breadth of discretion to schedule, assign, supervise and reward employees, and should do all of that within the auspice of the employee handbook. There are many classifications of employees in a workforce, for example full time versus part time, union versus non-union, etc. Each of these is generally covered by covenants within the handbook or other collective bargaining or legal agreements.

Policies and guidelines are constantly tweaked in today's business workplace. Managers and leaders communicate news and information to their workforce as often and in real time as warranted. It is important with the new electronic and instant communications techniques that the updates to policies and guidelines make it to the company doctrines as well as the handbook as soon as possible. Employees and managers should each have access to the handbook for on-demand reference. The days of print and distribution of updates are basically in the past and electronically signed policies should be centrally located and accessible.

Many businesses may not have the requisite resources to originate and keep the handbook updated as recommended above. What then? We feel that managers should read and understand the handbook for its tone and sentiment and always substitute logic, sensibility, humility and honesty into any administration of employee rights in lieu of a direct formula in the handbook.

Employee Benefits

Many important parts of the employee life cycle come at predictable times and some when least expected. These are generally covered under a benefits administrator. Start dates, on boarding and orientation, benefits enrollment, savings and investment selections, etc. are all examples of important early dates and usually scheduled and tracked. How can you, as a manager, support your workforce with professional administration of their other benefits, such as personal time off, extended medical leave, military leave, short or long term disability, family related leave, and so many other programs? Your workforce, who you are directly responsible for, will look to you as their immediate supervisor and more importantly, as their personal administrator. Benefits are extremely confusing to enroll in, place claims in and ultimately resolve life's issues. Your role may or may not be to provide administration on behalf of employees, but someone in your company does provide that. Perhaps the extent of that support is just connecting the workforce to a centralized or shared service which acts like a call center or help desk, but rest assured, your workforce depends on that.

Throughout the employee life cycle, there could be many assignment and organizational changes, and to the workforce, the expectations are the same from anyone they report to. Managers should stay as close to their HR partners and learn how to discern and disseminate benefits. An essential part of management is to keep a workforce engaged and motivated to work, clear on assignments and as free from distraction as possible. It would be a setback to handle benefits administration poorly and the workforce should be afforded a best chance to take advantage of this entitlement. This is another are that managers can collaborate and find value in the HR relationship and shared responsibility.

A very sensitive and critical phase of the life cycle is at the retirement stage. All of what an employee goes through to pick dates and set themselves up financially is just a small part of this life changing decision. You may be a new manager and someone on your staff is contemplating retirement. They may have been in the workforce for several decades and ready to dismount from the team. How prepared are you in case someone is in that stage on your team? Someone may move in from another division or company and soon afterwards starts the retirement planning protocol. Are you familiar with what this is and how to administer support?

Example of good benefits administration includes retirement because it is much more than just picking a date and setting up a financial plan. It may constitute one of the most personal and impactful decisions in one's life. Managers should be aware, and give opportunity to the retiring employee to set themselves up and offer as much support of time, contacts and services as possible. No one person has all the answers, but retirement planning includes so many phases, such as financial, health management, insurance coverage, emotional preparation and so on. As important as on boarding and orientation are to start on the right foot, retirement planning should be just as detailed and attended by managers. Work with your HR partners or search for the best practices to offer this phase as best in service.

Workplace Incidents

A major benefit to having a professional team available to handle certain instances of behavioral conduct is clearly centered around personal, harassment complaints. We won't delve very deeply into this sector of HR and management responsibilities as there are too many variables to find a single best solution. Current day incidents now require most companies need to have a certain protocol written into their handbook. There are steps every manager should take when someone claims they have been bullied, preyed upon, harassed, etc. Managers should be clear on what they need to do when first hearing or witnessing such an action or claim. Again, they should stay away from diagnosing and stick to documenting exactly what was expected, what action is alleged to have happened and allow the trained HR team or more senior leadership to take next steps. The most critical initial steps may be to hear, document and escalate the information in a timely manner. Should there be physical injuries evident, a second tier of responsibility will likely include administering emergency care protocols.

In some cases, your company may mandate that certain allegations require a second manager present during the initial conversation. Managers should be aware and use common senses when first investigating or discussing any claim. There are many opportunities for people in today's world to have recording devices, such as personal phones and eyewitness reports may often be complicated by playback of media. Managers should be as diligent as necessary, and document facts as required by your company's rules. Many cases are fairly dealt with when the information is available in an unbiased and professional report.

Another situation that managers should be fully aware of is the threat of workplace violence. There is no easy way to discuss the issue or softening of the topic. There are far too many violent or threatening incidents that could happen in a workplace. There are many situations in business workplaces and environments that need to take steps in security and safety and these procedures are led by the management teams. Know your place, understand your role in training through soft skills and you'll be a natural leader in spotting potential threats, recommending intervention steps and sustained security measures.

As a manager, your role may be best suited for early warning, real time reporting and follow up program management. How can you spot issues ahead of time, alert the right leadership or HR partners to step in and legally and especially ethically find solutions to protect your business? In most cases, the follow up forensics reveal gaps or missed signals that in retrospect seem obvious and stand out as the strings of declining behaviors and/or poor performance markers. The reviews foster discussions or opinions regarding future workplace rules or laws.

There are questions you should consider as a manager regarding workplace safety. Who is in your workforce, your workplace and your marketplace? Is your workplace and marketplace the same environment and are you overseeing safety and security for all? Examples would include schools, stores, daycare and senior centers, YMCA and Boys and Girls Clubs, public libraries and food establishments. These illustrate a wide spectrum of business and each may be just as vulnerable and therefore security should be in the oversight of sound management teams.

Your personal training with regards to workplace safety is important. There are ethical, compliant and legal guidelines in many industries and some are governed by local, state or federal law. Step up, get involved and be aware of these. Your responsibility to safety is a critical one. Once established as your company protocol, you may also implement change or train your workforce in their roles. The workplace and marketplace are incredibly complex ecosystems and often a crisis is triggered by something and a chain of events follows. Your role may be to lead steps to a safe conclusion, mitigating collateral damage and of course, reporting in real time and documenting activity. This will help create safer measures in future situations.

A very common program designed to keep workplace safe is a fire drill. Think of the life saving measures by simply following the rules in orderly fashion. Your role may be to ensure the success of the drill, meaning influencing your workforce to take it seriously, follow orders and prepare themselves to act accordingly should the real thing happen. Fire drills are one of many programs meant to promote safety, establish rules of crisis management and institutionally make the workforce aware that safety and security are paramount to success.

You may have an opportunity to develop plans and procedures that help to make the environments in which you employ or deploy a workforce to be safe, warm and welcoming.

Engagement with Workforce

Managing employee benefits starts during the recruitment stage and goes well into retirement. Personal benefits are very important to each employee and the Employee Advocacy engagement is important as a bond and trusted advisor for the workforce. The most personal interaction with the Employee Advocate (either HR or a business leader) is usually communications regarding benefits information and interpretation. That is a trait that all Employee Advocates must possess. They are expected to give straight talk in delivering a message and, in other cases, may have to untangle corporate structure or bureaucracy on behalf of an employee.

Engagement between the Employee Advocate and the employees or management is a critical part of the role. If the role is a centralized and inside Human Resources position, that professional has an advantage by determining the cadence of communication. The internal HR professional can update on topics that are either more familiar to or important overall personally to the workforce. Conversely, the external HR professional must rely on the inside management to handle much of the regular communication regarding policies, procedures and important workforce bulletins. Should this advocate role be part of a manager or leader/owner, they must balance their communication effectively to ensure messages are sent and received properly. In other words, don't mix the messages if you can help it. Some information will be widespread and corporate and some will be very individual and personally delivered. Leave no room for confusion or follow up to make sure the right reception of the message happened. It's critically important to stay engaged.

The manager or leader who also owns the Employee Advocacy role should decide both the cadence and discretion regarding on-going engagement and communication. Not all policy changes require full explanation, though some communication should point out the advantage or disadvantage of said change. Sell it and support it. People will all interpret messages slightly differently, so proper distribution and follow up procedures will work out well and the manager can decide how much additional information should accompany the message. The amount of transparency will flag the type of message and balance the expected reaction to it. The hybrid role of manager/Employee Advocate requires a delicate balance in the communications process.

Employee Assistance

Managers need to learn when, where and how to navigate the Employee Assistance protocol. Many companies employ, or partner with, an Employee Assistance Program (EAP). An EAP is a work-based intervention program designed to identify and assist employees in resolving their personal problems that may be adversely affecting their performance. This is where managers must learn to draw a line between handling personal behavior and performance. Behaviors are a science unto themselves and trained/certified professionals determine which behaviors are job related and which are resulting from other, personal conditions.

We need to make an important point concerning behavioral pattern changes in employees, ones that managers can usually witness. Draw the line here, as managers will observe, and should not attempt to diagnose the behavioral changes and personal conflict of individuals in the workforce. That diagnosis is left to clinically trained professionals. Managers should practice restraint and compliance and only report facts relating to the performance and results of the workforce. That's their territory for reporting. Facts and results. If new behaviors are observed and performance or expectations are changed as a result, a certified EAP professional should take on that case. It's defensible in court when a certified professional reports an opinion on behaviors.

Managers need to know the expectations of job related, behavioral habits, within their own company, and what appropriate steps to take in each case where change occurs. Behavioral steps, such as preparation, assignment hand off, communication protocol, reporting, time entry, shift status are examples of certain behaviors expected in specific business workplaces. It would be easy to spot something in an individual that affects performance. Managers should step back and follow the details of protocol. Many companies will follow some sort of escalating or progressive steps in handling personal issues. Documenting each conversation in a professional way and investigating issues properly are critically important to the EAP role. Some issues may get to a legal proceeding and that makes the early stages of documentation very significant to be accurate. The EAPA trains and certifies these professionals in how to properly handle situations. Workforce managers who properly document steps are more likely to ensure success in a case.

Many of these cases end up with some legal advising or process and must follow strict rules of engagement. The first expectation of a manager in resolving performance due to a change in habit, should be documenting only the facts. Among the common mistakes managers make include not documenting early and accurately a situation resulting in poor results, possibly due to an individual's change in behavior and performance. In many cases, managers cross a line and provide their own personal diagnosis of a condition, rather than sticking to the facts about the changes in work performance and subsequent results. For example, stating that an employee has not been performing up to performance expectations due to "*a family situation and stress*" is not within the defensible responsibilities of a workforce manager. Managers should leave the behavioral diagnosis out of the reports and documentation and an Employee Advocate or EAP professional can handle that. Workforce managers should stick to job roles, responsibilities and expectations and how an employee has not been delivering results in their performance. Facts pertaining to the workplace and individual job performance are enough to start an investigation and the process may then escalate to include personal support and rehabilitation of some sort.

Legal Advocacy

The Manager/Employee Advocate must be savvy in understanding some of the basics of labor law and legal responsibilities, as necessary, to conduct day to day business. For example, the basic information regarding federally protected status of time off or physical disability provisions should be part of the handbook. Any interpretation or challenge to these should be documented and legal partners brought in to help escalate requests, secure funding and/or resolve disputes. The Manager/EA role should be the first one to engage when there is something to mediate from the workplace and let them use good protocol in handling the sensitivity of it all.

There are tried and true procedures that seasoned managers are required to perform. The most common of these is progressive disciplinary procedures. It typically starts with a reporting of behavioral or performance related issues. These usually include addressing issues with all parties, setting ground rules or reiterating policy. Next, it is common to send out warnings or written warnings for repeat offenders. Should issues continue and the documentation is organized and thorough, likely a suspension and new terms, such as "leading up to and including termination" might accompany this step. Finally, should a firing be warranted, they engage the Human Resources and Legal team together to make the case and execute the orders. If the manager owns the EA role, he/she will deal directly with legal support. Depending on the company size, location and many other factors, certain levels of security and sustained personal protection are part of the termination process.

Whether the Employee Advocate role is inside or externally partnered, or perhaps you the manager owns the EA responsibilities as well, you must provide and expect the utmost of discretion and compliance when investigating, counseling, disciplining, policy changing, communicating or otherwise engaging your Human Resources team.

Empowering Staff Through Education

CHAPTER 5

Learning Never Gets Old

Successful companies understand how to train and upgrade their employee skill sets and competencies. They must do so to compete and win in such a demanding marketplace. Every industry offers challenges to member companies or manufacturers to keep up with technology, efficiencies and secure their future growth. In this section, we'll talk about the differences in learning and training and focus on areas such as comparing hard skills and soft skills.

The health of an organization can be directly related to its training processes and education of the workforce. A master plan is critically important to manage. Let's draw a line between education and training. An educated workforce is evidenced through vision, risk assessment, value proposition, employee engagement, wherewithal, vitality and culture. Training is best associated with technology, systems, operations, components, software or hardware enhancement, testing and workflow. Let's breakdown the nuances of Empowering Staff through Education.

Education

A basic philosophy for educating the workforce is that a company needs to inspire them both individually as well as collectively to seek out ways that make them smarter, relevant and more creative in their day to day role. Keeping up with the industry and the advances in technology, operating efficiencies and creative solutions to the normal operations will spark some to dig in and meet the challenges. Continuing education equips the workforce with contemporary thought and practice that they can incorporate into daily routines and resolve issues easier and more effectively.

Education and learning are available in many applications and formats. These include instructor led, on line, self-directed, certificate based, etc. Dependent upon the type of industry, company, role and available resources, a learning plan can offer a variety of solutions. Many parts of the continuing education plan may be inexpensive or even free of charge. These include the ability to "follow" companies and experts on line and on many types of social platforms such as LinkedIn and Facebook. These platforms offer a forum for thought leaders to share opinions and offer solutions, open conversations and share best practices. Often, a simple but direct question will garner a rich discussion and possible solutions. Many organizations, consulting companies and experts have dedicated followers. These are consumers who read the blogs and newsletters concerning specific industries they are either a part of, have affinity for or ones they aspire to join.

Employees at all levels will make themselves more valuable to their leadership by initiating their own personal growth through official educational channels. They will feel more engaged with the business if they keep up with industry trends and participate in workplace discussions with senior leaders on new standards and practices. There is a common learning plan that is credited to the Center for Creative Leadership (CCL) called *70-20-10*. The theory states that 70 percent of learning comes from on the job experience, 20 percent is attributed to coaching or mentoring (also known as developmental relationships) and the final 10 percent is specifically designated coursework or formal training regimen. As the workforce applies new theories and creative thinking to their roles, the education can pay off as they will feel more entrepreneurial. https://www.ccl.org/articles/leading-effectively-articles/70-20-10-rule/

For these purposes, we'll try and make a distinction between the terms learning and training. Learning can happen anytime and anyplace when something is introduced into a situation that changes or advances one's repertoire. Training is more regimented, predictable and calculated. It comes in forms such as end-user training, whereby a manual and component, equipment or system is paired with or without a second, more experienced trainer and the user goes through step by step processing. Today's training may take on more creative processing, though the theories remain the same, that for each advance in technology or systems generated, more time and practice is required to get the controls and usage correct. A basic style is known as *on the job* training. In many cases, observing and participating in an operable mode makes the best option for someone to learn a new component, system or workplace change. There is a direct correlation of training to the bottom line. The quicker the training, the more valuable the workforce.

Training programs are successful when the workforce is engaged and understand the expectations. Good trainers are worth their weight in gold. Simply, they get results when they understand the timelines and their trainees, how to best apply training criteria, disseminate feedback, assessment and testing. There are many other great qualities to look for in your trainers and trainees. Training for job related skills and operations are usually left to a business unit or the line of business to execute while other learning can be negotiated and/or collaborated with an HR team as a business objective. Many business leaders purchase and implement new equipment or systems because there is an expectation of efficiency, reliability and relevant success. None of it can be realized unless the staff has access to train on it and be comfortable in delivering products and services in a timely and measurable new routine. The HR led training is generally associated with protecting the brand or company assets, such as compliance guidelines, sexual harassment training, workplace safety, social media policies and safe harbor style training.

For a verification exercise, create a list of the various types of learning and training that are available or prevalent in your business. Try to place the various programs into either a learning or a training bucket. Whatever the balance, it sums up to empowering the staff through education.

Components

The components of empowering through education will differ between industries and companies. Every company has unique needs for education and the respective learning and training components will be keys to success. There is some common ground in all companies, each must figure out the proportion of learning and training and map it into your master plan.

Most companies create or manufacture something to sell and therefore place a value on their services or output. This is true for media companies which create content for consumption (news, weather, sports, etc.) as well as steel factories forging metals to create beams for construction of bridges and/or sandwich shops who feed people daily. If there is a supply chain to create an output or solution, then learning and training is important to implement.

Let's look at an example of how education plays a role in a particular business. In a restaurant, the dishwasher is indirectly connected to the maître d. Therefore, each position plays a vital role in the business plans. The dishwasher must learn the compliant steps in health and cleanliness standards. He/she has workflow training on the various systems that must be used in the routines of the job. As the dishwasher learns and becomes more proficient and reliable, perhaps more on the job training (observing others) is available and a next step could include supporting the wait staff or apprentice kitchen work. Both learning and training become components of the plan for the dishwasher. Eventually, the role may lead to taking more responsibility and gaining background and experience towards becoming a person in charge or perhaps a future maître d. The maître d has likely come through a multiple step background which includes learning about customer service and the specialties of a front-end food and hospitality business. As this person continues to strive or evolve further, that dishwasher is gaining his/her own experience and education towards moving up. Both are essential to the workflow and therefore success of the operation.

Horizontal and Vertical Training

Most workers are genuinely interested in advancing their careers and curious about other roles. Many want to know what is similar or different about the jobs across the bench or down the line from them. This is also part of the *horizontal learning*, simply knowing what's further out in the division, company or industry at similar levels to yourself. Often the core skills or competencies may be similar for the roles to the left or right of your own role. Likely, the hard skills would be different for a role in operations versus a similarly paid role in administration or marketing. These are different industry roles, though similarly placed in a compensation grid. Often the opportunities for advancement may start with a lateral move before a vertical one is a possibility.

Many employees think it's important to know what they are missing and how to bridge the gap, (through learning and training), to a promotion. Sometimes, the roles to your left or your right might be a jumping off point for someone who is interested in trying a different career path, with at least fifty percent of the skill set or core competencies already successfully demonstrated. It's not always that easy to move laterally first, though it's human nature to think there's something better in the wings. These are conversations and decisions that managers and their workforce must engage in.

The more dedicated a company is to the retention of a workforce, engaged in this manner, the better the chance for measurable advances and a good company culture. The culture has many other components necessary, such as diversity, strong communication and employee engagement. It's also important for the workforce to learn about the company culture and add to it.

Soft Skills versus Hard Skills

The soft skills are often referred to as competencies. These are usually defined by the type of business capability or talent that deal with ensuring success. It's usually something from within a person, a drive, a belief or a personality trait that sparks the process and lights the fire of competence. A common phrase to describe someone in this regard is "results driven". That term is easily understood, yet you still need contextual evidence, facts or data to support the case being made. Within the competency of "results driven" there are generally 4-6 components of escalating ability or expectation, to set personal goals appropriately and deliver them. Think of other terms such as "team building", "diversity", "communication", "leadership", etc., and see how they may differ or get more intense as the workforce gains experience and sets higher expectations for themselves. Soft skills round out a professional.

The hard skills are directly related to the job at hand, usually found in the operational roles. Systems and procedures generally call for strict adherence and repetition. Roles that require a manual or step by step protocol will have hard skills training and the more refined one gets in their ability to produce results, the more the soft skills will influence success. Hard skills are easier to measure than soft skills, and transferable in many cases. Managers should break down roles by each of these types of skills to assess overall performance and set expectations accordingly.

How is education and/or training delivered and why are the various methods so important? First, you must understand some of the differences in hard skills and soft skills. Let's take an example from a livery service company. There is the front-end sales and customer service professional who can fit you into the right vehicle with the right driver and the right type of amenities. That person is likely using soft skills to sell, market, strategically schedule, set expectations and provide a satisfied experience. Meanwhile, the driver has taken lessons regarding physical presentation, communication, vehicle performance, has practiced driving, parking and navigating in all types of traffic situations and returning the customers and vehicles successfully. These represent various hard skills at work.

All employees must perform. Some will contribute to and/or create physical products or services. Many others may be offering consultative services and selling, marketing or delivering presentations to support the company. The balance of roles that are individual contributor type will generally have more hard skills and the sales or management level will have more soft skills or competencies to draw from. There are always exceptions to this theory, usually based on the size of a company where certain staff take on many roles.

Management Roles and Setting Expectations

The role of management at all levels in learning and training should start as entrepreneurial and inspirational. No better method than role modeling and leading by example. Create the environment for educating and/or training and foster, nurture and cultivate it. Value the process and ensure a return on investment of the people who participate. Managers can usually influence their senior leaders to support training and influence resources, including budgets, to invest in learning plans and training programs. Some of these can be efficiently and creatively worked out, such as reducing travel costs by encouraging webinars or bringing one trainer or consultant in versus sending a dozen or more staff out of house for training.

Set your expectations to deliver results, if you spend the money or time to get your staff more training, make sure you follow up. This is a good way to show the engagement and trust that is required for the company to support such an effort. It ensures a mutual trust. If you outsource this initiative to an HR partner or outsourced firm, how engaged are they with your plan and are they supporting your communications and master plan surrounding any employee learning or training event?

Steer the education and training to hold true to that master plan. Your role as a manager is a good opportunity to weave learning and training into a performance plan, evaluate the effort and results and make the engaged workforce feel more valued. The action steps associated with rolling out a good master plan and sustaining it will yield a good mark for workforce satisfaction, retention, management interaction and company culture.

What makes the workforce stronger through a good master plan of education and training will ultimately strengthen the management as well. They also need to stay ahead of their competition and know they will be managing a smarter and more effective workforce. Understand how to manage people better, keep those managers training to engage, inspire, set expectations and assess effectively, even with a more advanced workforce. Don't let the curve pass them by. Always communicate and organize the feedback. It's essential to foster communication and circle back and forth through surveys and 360 feedback to ascertain best practices.

Benefits and Consulting

Finally, the expectations of a good master plan should yield strong results. If the plan needs to be trimmed or cut based on economic or other factors, have the overall scope of it understood and try to inspire and achieve the same results, albeit in an abbreviated fashion. Good communication regarding tightening of resources can still help in satisfaction and productivity for your staff. They are proportionally being trained by what resources are available, it's that simple. Your soft skills in setting expectations will help you communicate messages and results to your staff and engage them in doing what's best in any situation. You are empowering them with learning and training tools and they should in turn be building a better workforce. That's a simple way to calculate results. It's a true ROI to the empowerment of the workforce through education.

CHAPTER 6

A Healthy Business is Always Recruiting

The life cycle of a hire starts well before the candidate ever becomes an employee. Managers and leaders should always have a detailed understanding of the parameters of the roles they both supervise and hire for. This helps when it comes to sourcing good talent. There are many specific components that we look for in candidates and we'll discuss those later when we cover the "intake" meetings. For now, let's go through the timelines and milestones necessary to source talent, collect and disseminate data and select the best candidates for the jobs we employ.

Always Recruiting

Managers should always be recruiting, with or without open positions to fill. Business changes often and roles and responsibilities along with it. Technology, automation, sales, etc. are examples of systems and/or processes that can change business quickly and therefore leaders should remain flexibly open to alter their staffing requirements. Change often requires a staffing shift or modifying roles. Filling a roster is a basic step of managing, while motivating them to grow and prosper is a competency of good leadership. Often, the best candidates to fill an open role may already be on their roster and leadership should consider looking within to compare the qualifications of best in the workforce against external candidates. This internal recruiting activity allows a company to create a culture of good will, growth and development. Workforce is buoyed by management who take care in developing talent.

Always recruiting is a good state to be in. Leaders should be looking at other businesses within their industries and learning more about the best practices regarding workforce management. They should know where the best candidates come from and how skilled or experienced they are, no matter the level or skills necessary for the roles. Job Fairs, Veterans' programs and college campuses are examples of workforce breeding ground. Let's focus on the life cycle of hiring.

Hiring Process Starts with a Vacancy

There are many reasons that lead to *creating a vacancy* in your organization. These may include starting a new business, someone leaving the company, someone getting a promotion, expanded business coming in and many others. We won't go into validating any of the decisions to create the vacancy, just assume for this exercise it is legitimate. Your company should have a process that launches a recruitment and hiring initiative to fill the vacancy. As a manager, this is one of the most important initiatives you will work through. The decision to place someone in a role both fills a business need and affects people and process. Leaders must balance the priorities of a business and having the critical roles filled is an essential element to success. Otherwise, a hole in the roster can be inefficient and costly. There is a certain amount of work and expectations in any role, and especially apparent in a vacant role, so the quicker you fill it, the better the business will be, correct? Not necessarily.

In many companies, the recruitment process, (aka talent acquisition), may be outsourced to a staffing agency, partnered with an internal Human Resources Recruiter or left to the manager, owner and/or administrative leader. For our purposes, let's agree that the role is yours, the manager. In any way, the process is very similar from a larger company to a smaller one, albeit with less handoffs to an HR partner or outsourced party.

Your role may be to source, select and bring on board the best candidate and aptly fit for your team. Once there, managing and motivating that employee (re-recruiting) can be part of your ongoing role. It all starts with a vacancy. The vacancy represents a role with specific qualifications and expectations. The process should be clearly laid out and calculated, whether the job is for an easy position to fill or a strategic search for a very special skill set. Your vacancy might be for a true entry level position with little to no qualifications other than age and availability. Or, your role could be for a very highly skilled or experienced specialist of some kind. Either way, a good employee, a good fit for your business, should be your goal.

The very decision to approve the vacancy and start recruitment supports normal business objectives. The manager should have a sound understanding of the role and requirements so it can be posted for hire with accuracy and confidence. The job description is a critical document. Therefore, when describing the vacant role, pay attention to the true qualifications, both basic and strategic, the required background, experience, education and any other motivating criteria to round out your plan to fill it. The vacancy, now paired with a proper job description, should take on certain personality characteristics. Your posting and job description are important to be comparable. Your decision on final selection is important for your business. This organization early in the process will allow you to pick candidates who best match the stated criteria for role, not the other way around. Best selections are therefore made without bias and easily defended.

There is a saying that often "the answer was hiding in plain sight". Sometimes your best candidate may already be a part of your organization. That all depends on your business and specific roles. Comparisons are a constant in the recruitment process, so evaluating internal and external candidates may be a good routine. Take the time to learn the business roles and org charts so you can see where the internal candidate pool may come from. Then create a vacancy.

Business leaders need to do things orderly and in compliance. Filling the roster is no exception. As noted earlier, your recruitment may be done internally by the Talent Acquisition group in HR, externally by agency or possibly by you, the business leader, manager or owner. In every case, there are certain rules and laws that must be followed and accounted for. Certainly, good organizational detail in the recruitment process will pay off in the end.

Intake

An important early stage of recruitment happens at the intake meeting. Whether the hiring manager is the sole owner of the recruitment or has a full team internally or externally to manage the process, the manager must fully understand what is expected at the conclusion. The best hire for the role should ultimately be the manager's decision, with help and support along the way, where applicable. Intake is the first official meeting of the vested parties to discuss all the parameters of a new vacancy and subsequent hiring strategies. Setting expectations is a critical process. For example, some questions to consider include: where to source from, what's the budget, how many qualified candidates would make a good pool to choose from, how long do we expect to take on each step of the way, how will we communicate and what's in it for each of the vested parties?

The sourcing strategy is important as it deals with where, when and how to search, such as job or industry boards, colleges, niche organizations, job aggregators, company career sites, etc. This is also part of a process known as strategic sourcing, which takes a well-defined role and further evaluates through screening, interviewing and/or testing the important requirements such as a specific skill set or demonstrated bundle of competencies. A posting may have a cascading array of skills, education or other requirements and the hiring manager can assign a weight or a qualification filter to determine what the minimum threshold would be to qualify a candidate to advance in the process. Strategic sourcing is meant to be impactful and not time consuming. It allows the manager built in filters to make decisions efficiently.

Sourcing and recruitment can be effective if run similarly to a project timeline. For example, how often will you refresh the posting and how should it be marketed to maximize its potential? These and many more questions should be noted in an outline and agreed to by all parties. Templates for intake meetings can usually be found in good recruiter blogs or sites on the internet. Customize these outlines to each job to gain a greater understanding of the process and interdependence on the others involved in the talent acquisition process.

Sourcing involves searching for the pools of candidates for the specific jobs and marketing directly to them. Often, candidates may be personally referred from any number of sources, including peers, subordinates, friends, relatives, college administration and company executives. Be careful when accepting the referrals and make sure there is a clear understanding of each role in that process. You may accept a referral, but be clear on what the next steps are, is there an expectation of a screening, interview or actual placement into a role? Don't get stuck with a lesser candidate, referred to you, if you can help it. Some of the process may be out of your control, for example, perhaps the CEO sends you a referral and asks you to find a role for the person. Have a written policy for all employees, including managers and executives, on how the referrals process can work. It will be well worth the effort.

Perhaps the most intriguing element of intake is the discussion around a budget for the hiring process. The budget for hiring will vary by role, company, location, and could include any targeted marketing or expenses incurred for traveling candidates to or from interviews, etc. It's important to get as much information up front and especially know who is signing off on budget approvals. Who manages that budget will be held accountable, so your role may involve either spending or approvals or both. For some roles, outsourcing the candidate search function could become very expensive compared to normal recruitment, but worth the effort for niche or hard to fill positions. Sourcing strategy is a good conversation at intake to have with anyone associated with decisions regarding a hire. Communication is very important in the recruitment process. Ultimately, a very detailed and open communication plan is a key factor for success, including any budget related items. There should be a budget, a timeline and a cadence of communication established at the intake meeting.

Make Your Job Posting Sing

Posting an open position is a key early step. There are numerous ways to simply "post" an open position. Postings may go up on internal/external communications, job boards, industry blogs, social media platforms and many other alternatives. The job posting is the marketplace announcement of the open position, with the specific requirements listed. Remember, the vacancy was approved based on business needs. The requirements for filling that vacancy should be clearly stated as well as the expectations for the person who occupies it. All candidates should be evaluated against consistent expectations or requirements to have a fair and balanced approach to filling a specific role, no matter the level.

If the posting and required attributes are clear, add some key information about the company and market it. The type of information added to each posting should be about the company, it's locations, culture, history, current news, etc. A paragraph or two to introduce the company at the beginning of the posting and a couple short ones to end the posting are important. It can show carefully worded information that takes some of the mystery out or just adds consistency to the posting so that all postings from your company look professionally and creatively aligned. This shows good employer branding to prospects. This combination of information works well together and makes the environment, the workplace, the culture and the role all align. This is your shot at attracting the best candidates and hopefully filtering out those applicants who are not qualified and won't waste your time and resources.

Posting is the public marketing of a role that is open for candidates to bid on. The simple posting process is not always glamorous. Consider some of the steps discussed at the intake meeting. From that collaboration, the interview and selection team's specific roles should be carefully considered, such as where to post and how to respond to the flow of traffic based on where and when it gets activity. This is important to note. Any member of the selection team can have an elevated role based on when candidate flow starts. Keep consistent communication channels open.

Branding is important to understand. There's a difference between company and employer branding and the best companies work to meld these brands to maximize their collective strengths. Company brand usually includes a business strategy and language to move content, products and services. An employer brand is how a company markets for their workforce. It may include statements or inference regarding culture and people, growth and development, etc. It is meant to attract people to a business, location and environment to work, not to find consumers to shop. Savvy consumers and candidates each can weigh the brand identities.

While posting a role is a basic step to the hiring process, *marketing* a role takes it to another level. Marketing should be more strategic, creative and certainly targeted. Years ago, a company might post a role on a job board and hope the right candidates would be looking for it and apply. Many referred to that as "post and pray". Today, with social media, passive candidates (those not necessarily searching for a new role) are targeted ahead of time and many are made aware of jobs and opportunities while they are feeling comfortable in current conditions. Marketing may include providing candidates with substantive information regarding the state of their industry which may pique interest about what may come (downsizing, mergers and acquisitions, for example) that they may have not previously considered. This method of sourcing candidates is important as the pace of business and change today requires businesses to stay aware of talent pools and specialists, just in case a situation comes up where a replacement is needed.

Marketing today is a very creative function, and some ways, the monetary rewards of a role are marketed to a candidate to keep them interested or get them to accept an offer. Some roles are laden with incentives that could include sign on bonuses, relocation services and/or other amenities. For our discussion, we'll let you investigate what rewards and/or cultural perks your company makes available through the talent acquisition process.

On the other hand, it's a good idea to continue to re-recruit the best of your own workforce, keep tabs and open dialogue so they know exactly where they stand on your team in case an external recruiter should come calling for them. Your workforce may be doing well and will not know specifically how you feel about them individually unless you talk to them. Keeping an on-going and open dialogue is a good practice and engagement is a great way to keep your staff interested and invested in your business, not someone else's. Good communication is a hallmark of best performance management as well. That leads individuals on your staff to want to stay and do well for you, the manager. This practice of internally re-recruiting the best of your staff may be an opportunity for someone to know how well they are judged, valued and appreciated at home. By keeping an open line of communication, you may be able to help your staff see other opportunities in your business, perhaps a role that you could help them with instead of them looking outside the company.

Aggregator Sites, Screening and Tracking Systems

There are many options as to where to post open jobs and attract interest. Many on-line websites cater to the recruitment process and candidates must be aware of the preponderance of them and decide which of them to trust. Many don't originate job postings, they scrape other sites and re-post jobs to intercept the normal flow of employer to candidate and these steps tend to confuse the issue. Both manager and candidate need to be aware of the recruitment landscape and expect there to be confusion in the early stages of the process. Managers should understand that candidates are often pulled in to these websites and sometimes don't really know how they were first found or contacted. If your company has a career site, you can direct any applicant or ask your recruiter to steer applicants to your career site for their profile and application. This keeps things very organized for your legal tracking. If you use third party sites or agencies to post jobs, pay attention to where they post them. There may be legal guidelines regarding the advertising of certain roles, so be aware if there are any regulations set forth before you launch a posting.

When your posting goes up and/or out, many candidates may be interested, and that number may be much more than you have anticipated. Will you be required to screen all of them to find the best one? How will you know when the best one has been found? You need to stay disciplined and organized and set some parameters ahead of time. If you have a smaller company and do the recruitment and staffing yourself, use these stages as a guide and keep your process orderly and information filed appropriately. Remember, with so many forms of electronic communication and storage, the life cycle of recruitment is more vulnerable if you don't keep it a separate and significant project, managed closely. Reminder that candidate data is confidential.

There are several methods to sorting through profiles, resumes and applications. For popular jobs, based on a large interest, it could be impossible to screen through all applicants to find the best ones. Recruitment process has come a long way and the applicant tracking systems (ATS) can help that process. Key word or phrases from the job posting are just one simple way to electronically scan for qualified and legitimate applicants. Weighting the job requirements (such as higher priority on experience versus education, for example), can help sort out which applications are closer to your intended selections There are many reasons to use good applicant tracking systems and in some cases, federal laws and guidelines prevail.

Audit reports are essentially good practice to show the process, diligence, decision making and resolution. These reports help to ensure better results each time.

Sometimes it's difficult to start the process of recruiting. You have a vacancy and need to fill it with a qualified, motivated and reliable person. No matter the role, the level or the location, your selection must also be qualified, motivated and reliable. A good starting place would be to create the role virtually and look at it from many points of view, such as how it handles information dissemination, customer service, interactions with vendors, public speaking, sales calling, etc. Figure out the ideal "virtual" candidate for your job and build a mock profile. Make sure it fits into your organizational chart and the skills and background necessary for it is aligned with the roles around it. How much motivation would it take for the right person to show up every day and be successful in the role? You can now put a job description together or validate an existing one, create a job posting that is effective and set expectations for the role, before recruiting on it.

Utilizing social media allows an additional strategy to finding targets. Recruiters, managers and employees who have social media accounts can forward links to jobs and they can all ask their friends and followers to gauge interest or continue to send out. Many services, such as LinkedIn, aggregate account holders categorically and this helps to send the right messages out in many cases to a filtered audience. Targeted marketing and recruiting is key. This makes it a better chance of landing a fish where you know they are in that right body of water!

Once the posting has been established, what types of questions will garner the best answers to compare with all candidates applying? What specific answers are you looking for? The goal is to not only ask the best questions but to ascertain the best answers you're looking for and keep that consistent with all the candidates. Now you have the foundation for a very fair and balanced process. That's the start of an organized process, which is an important way to recruit because all roles are not filled with one solution. There are many ways to recruit and fill a roster spot. Identify the role and start there. Perhaps your role is not as demanding and requires little to no background or education. Even at that step, you should be assessing based on the motivation of the candidates to land that job. Who can express themselves in the way that suits your business plan in the best way should win. If the role is a specialized or executive one, the predetermined questions and answer guides will be very important to use as a navigational tool through the interview and selection process.

A preferred process of mine is a structured interview, such as taught to me by the team at Development Dimensions International (DDI), a management consulting company several years ago. https://www.ddiworld. com/ Let's look briefly at four areas that you should consider for screening and analysis that will filter the best candidates to the top of your lists for final selection. Screening a resume/profile/application is a best practice to start the filter. Education, skills, experiences and motivation are areas that can separate the field of candidates and produce final selections. The ones who best match the requirements as posted get moved forward and those that fall short are disqualified. Initial screening should validate credentials, *as a candidate*, not necessarily a final selection. Education requirements, basic skills and years of experience can be vetted efficiently through a variety of methods and save time and resources. Perhaps an electronic scanning, phone calls or resume review gets you through to the applicants you consider the best of the bunch.

For our understanding, applicants are generally regarded as *anyone* who simply applies to a posted role and the *candidate* status is based on being basically qualified for the role. Posting a job with exact requirements (qualifications, background, experiences, education, other motivating factors, etc.) makes it easy to surface best candidates. The posting reflects the role that should have a job description which is accurate and defensible. Why is that important? When someone is hired to a specific job, there are in most cases, scores of candidates who believe they were the best fit for that role. Every so often, managers or business leaders are challenged in court for their decisions because the job market is so competitive. The business leaders should take the steps to document their stages of hiring and decisions made, to defend their final decisions and protect the integrity of the process and business as well. Some roles may attract a flood of applicants and it takes time to screen through everything. There are electronic screening programs for higher end sourcing and at some point, human touch as well. Either way, the applicant tracking system (ATS) should report the posting, the pool and how the elimination of applicants works all the way to final selection stage. This is how you can defend your decision.

Stages and the Candidate Experience

There are many ways to begin *filtering candidates* down to a final list from which to select from. Screening resumes and reviewing job applications is a good first step. Make sure the basics are covered. Many businesses leave this early step in the hands of outsourced vendors or perhaps a part of the administrative support staff. It is, nonetheless, an important stage and sets up the team for success. There may be some information uncovered through screening resumes, such as a college degree or certification discrepancy or perhaps an unusual way to calculate years of experience. A brief conversation to sort that out can be a valuable step before committing time and resources to an in-person interview. It's very important to take good contemporaneous notes and compare each candidate for best answers. It ensures that the process runs smoothly.

Once your candidate list has been brought to a reasonable number, set aside the resumes and create a list of questions that each candidate will answer over the phone. These screening questions are important. They represent a formal stage in the process of filtering candidates. The phone screens are ways to engage early questions and fact checking with candidates. Some of the questions here should be to verify the basic qualifications, such as education, years of experience, current or most recent employment, basic role and availability. The questions should be fundamental in nature, to weed out information that satisfies basic requirements and further qualifies candidates. They should not get too involved in hard skills assessing or in motivation. There must be consistency in the questions asked so the process is fair and balanced when moving the best candidates forward.

Phone screening begins a personal relationship with a candidate, so understand the dynamic. The candidate is excited to hear from a human in the process and will be very anxious to hear about any updates on progress regarding themselves in the recruitment process. Candidates know they are in competition and you should set appropriate expectations of what happens next. If you are on the recruiting end and initiating screening calls, make sure the candidate knows that they are amongst others and as the selection process gets underway they will either be moved forward in the process or dismissed. You or someone designated will be their contact.

Don't be afraid of that call to dismiss someone, even though it's a tough one, because it makes you stronger to be able to give that information back to a candidate in a professional and measured tone. Some managers and recruiters will write down or script some of the language to ensure that message is fair and consistent. Remind the candidate of their initial call when you stated you would be their messenger, with good or bad news and continue. It's also a good practice not to explain too much about what they are missing in your judgment and stating only that those remaining candidates, who are moving ahead, more closely matched thee job as posted. That's all you need to leave them with. Always close out candidates with professional courtesy. It's ultimately an unbiased and defensible statement.

Recruiting relies on chemistry. You as a recruiting manager, whether you hire or dismiss candidates, will be respected for your professional approach to each person you connect with throughout the process. Consistency is the best practice in the recruiting and staffing field. Keep your screening answers organized so you can easily refer to them and as often as necessary.

Own the Interview

The interview is the most important stage. Both sides are vested in this process and need to be at their very best to make it work successfully. Managers need to practice questioning and listening carefully to answers. Remember the candidate is also evaluating you, your role and your participation in their very personal journey. It's also a good practice to set the stage when you first sit down, allowing both of you to have share the experience and be comfortable. What type of questions will you cover, what part of the candidate's background will you be interrogating and how much time do you expect to take. Set expectations up front, ask if the outline of your meeting is understood and if there are any other questions they might have ahead of time. These are just a few suggestions, so it's a good idea to take the role seriously and own it. Be prepared!

If a candidate is moving forward from the phone screening and coming on site for an interview, take time to showcase your company, culture and the best candidate experience. The in-person interview stage is very important for both sides to up their game and nail the day. The candidate experience with regards to traveling in for an on-site interview should be well thought out and inspiring. Think of ways to integrate other staff, facility tours, possibly lunch or other events to make the day memorable. Interviews are important on both sides of the table. Each side is "auditioning" the other. The candidate is vying for the role and the interviewer to showcase the work, the team and the culture. Each has vested interests throughout the process.

Worth noting to anyone on the interview team is they should comprehend where the candidate is at any stage. Candidates are anxious and might need some time to think between questions, trying to put their best effort into every answer. A candidate will rehearse questions and answers, likely having spent time preparing themselves and doing anything they can to demonstrate the best abilities to perform in the job. You, as an interviewing manager and any others who assist you in that capacity, should also understand how important your role is in showcasing the best of your team and company. Don't fall short and show up unprepared or you run the risk of losing the best candidates and the process will fail. A key role for any manager, owner or leader is to own this process, because recruiting talent to come onto the business, to stay in the business and to advance in the business is a key ingredient of success. Re-recruiting your best workforce starts with the best talent coming in to interview.

Organization is a hallmark of good management. Structured interviewing is a very definitive and scientific approach. How well do you know the role you need to fill? How specific is the job description? How closely related are the job description and job posting? Have you reviewed each of these key documents so you know what the candidate is also expecting? If the answers are all acceptable to these questions, you should be ready to prepare for the interview. A key early step to organizing your interview is to create question and answer guides, directly related to specific jobs and use these templates with each candidate. Your goal is to ask consistent questions and note answers that most closely resemble your prescribed answers. You can also use other motivational or other experience keys to weigh differences between the best candidates. The structured approach is a non-bias and proven method for selecting the best candidate.

A best practice of structuring your interview involves breaking down each job into areas of specific focus that will add up to thorough coverage. These areas include knowledge, skills, experience and motivation. Break down your job into these areas and create questions that will uncover answers to the basic requirements and again, ask these consistently of each candidate. A good practice is also to build the posting in similar respect to the job description and aligns the language, expectations and clarity of who you source and will eventually manage.

As the jobs become increasingly more advanced and/or you are required to interview many candidates, you might have the chance to involve others in the interview process. There are various ways to set up interviews. Perhaps you have a team to interview each candidate. Can you ensure that each member of that team is qualified to ask the right questions and qualified to interpret each answer? A structured practice will assign specific areas of the interview process to interview team members and use the same question/answer templates with each candidate. This method ensures fair and thorough coverage of knowledge, skills, experience and motivation for each candidate in your process.

Set a weight on some areas of assessing candidates so you know what can be overcome with training or coaching, versus what someone might lack in experience and might require too much attention or supervision to upgrade. This takes the guess work out in selection. Interpreting the data after each interview through a conversation with the interviewers and having the interview process owner as the coordinator will keep it all compliant and balanced. Integrate the answer data and score each interview to compare and/or contrast best candidates.

After your teams have exhausted their investigative roles, when the candidates have been all reviewed, screened and/or interviewed, the interviewing team should get together and discuss the similarities, differences and what set the best ones apart. There are ways to score those answers and it brings a very non-bias approach to evaluating the candidates. How close did each candidate come to answering similarly to your anticipated results? The closer they answered, the better their individual scores. The best answers will help you select the best candidates for hire. A good debate is critical as each interviewer gets to input based on fact, answers and can compare candidates in a fair way.

Now you should be ready to select a final candidate and go through the compensation steps of creating an offer and explaining the total rewards to your finalist. This is a critical step. In lieu of or alongside an HR partner, make sure you have a template for the speaking points of your offer and write everything down, it's very important to have a good offer delivery to your finalist. Expect there to be several questions and a back and forth period of discussion. There are numerous variables in this stage from both sides. Towards the end of the interview with each candidate, expect questions from them about salary, environment, bonus, advancement, etc. from them. It's natural for candidates to inquire about any number of areas they feel would benefit them. Listen carefully, take notes if necessary and only answer what you are 100% sure of. It's a good idea not to let on any leaning, to or from, a candidate at the interview stage as something may invariably complicate your decision. Best to leave that stage with an opportunity to further investigate and then make a most informed decision when the rest of the facts and discussion are in. If you can, set a timetable to re-connect with an update or leave the candidate with your contact information or someone on the team to field additional questions.

Make an Offer and Close

Recruiters are trained to negotiate and close the deal, like sales professionals. Think of selling a house. If you get an agent to market and close it for you, they will take care of the finer compliant details and have your back. A prospect may offer lower than your price and want to negotiate for upgrades, fixtures, maybe kitchen appliances. You have every right to add or subtract from your price to satisfy that balance. Think of the real estate agent as your HR recruiter. The agent understands taxes, legal fees, procedures and closing protocol. Similarly, the Recruiter will know more about benefits, personnel rights and maybe even 401(k) matching or unpaid options that could be valuable to the candidate.

Total rewards encompass all value options for hiring someone. If there is any flexibility there, managers should understand the total rewards piece. During the offer and closing stages a candidate may try to extend whatever benefit they can to start with, such as higher pay, bonus or incentive plan, more vacation time, guaranteed travel, training, expense accounting, etc. Perhaps a one-time sign on bonus, a relocation package, upcoming tuition reimbursement or other benefit is worth discussing at time of offer. You need to know what is within your role as a manager or as an interviewer to engage in this type of discussion and how to handle it. Recruiters or seasoned managers have been through this scenario in the past. Learn how they do it, not over promising, but talking through your rewards, such as offering potential growth or perhaps a great company culture to enrich with. Research what your company may have to add and/or offer.

Keep Investigating

The background and reference checks are well worth the effort for the hiring team. A good background check will validate areas such as education, criminal history, work experience, perhaps credit history, etc. This should be done with anyone you decide to move forward and make an offer to. Your offer should be made *contingent upon a successful background check* so if there is any hint of impropriety or misleading information, you can pull the offer back without rebuttal. Your business can be protected by a sound background checking system. The background check is a simple and effective process. If you have an international or visa sponsored candidate, make sure you have the HR and/or legal support to ensure compliance and protocol. It ensures that any document or answer has been legally or professionally vetted by an external process and confidence in successful hiring is ensured. There are many instances of checks and balances that companies use in investigating candidates for hire and many more hiring practices require specific rules, laws and compliance. It is yours and your company's responsibility to either know and comply by them or hire the appropriate HR or counsel to ensure it.

A reference check is a separate and often effective procedure. It will generally use statements from peers, subordinates or former managers about what the person was like to work with, for or be managed. A good reference check is endorsed by the candidate, as they have the most to benefit. They ask for immediate action by those requested to input on their behalf. This is more of a behavioral assessment of working with, for or managing them in the past. If there were issues, a savvy reference check may root something out and throw a red flag up for the hiring manager. It allows for further dialogue or investigation that could result in a pivot from that candidate as the final selection. It's another step in the practice of hiring the best candidates for your business.

Bring it Home

On Boarding is a very important part of the life cycle. You've landed your candidate and he/she is now coming to work as a new employee. What will be their first impression as a hire? They should have had a good hiring experience and now the on boarding is critical to get right. Create a list of the important items you should present to a new hire. Many compliance and legal forms are required in the on boarding process. Your business may have special procedures for getting these filled and processed appropriately. Get to know this important step. New technologies and secure measures allow for most on boarding documentation to be done via internet. It allows for secure transfer of personal information such as legal status and government identification. This is a step in efficient process, to spend quality time when the new hire starts in the orientation of them and acclimation to the team and company versus filling out paperwork and having personal identification handed out and copied.

The items in the on boarding packet may include a welcoming letter from a strategic person (executive, owner, etc.), information on your pay, benefits, company policies or handbook, organizational chart or equivalent, etc. When the new hire starts, set up tours, training, meet and greets with key team members or management, etc. Plan the first 30-60-90 days with your new hires as necessary to provide a thorough on boarding experience. Some companies have formal or official orientation programs, filled with information, cultural experiences, training programs and historical data for new hires. New hires welcome them and learn about company ideals and expectations. Depending on the size and scope of your company, find out what you do and if there is room to improve your on-boarding procedures to ensure the best start possible for new hires.

Every instance of hiring should tie back to an established life cycle for recruitment whereby the company has a defined path with service level agreements, time allowances, strong communication and stage or process owners. Bottom line is that the recruiters should understand the full life cycle of the process. They need to impart that on hiring managers and the management teams should rely on the recruiters to own that process. A typical life cycle may include, but not be limited to: creating a vacancy, posting/marketing, candidate filtering, phone screening, sending to manager for screening, interviewing, selecting finalists, gaining approvals, verbal offering, checking background and references, written offer, acceptance, data processing and on boarding.

There are many other conditions that occur in some companies. They may include international hiring, or simply that a new hire may require a special work visa to work in the US. We won't go into depth in this scenario, just know that there are many varieties of visas for different situations and legal processes that must be followed for each of these hires. See your legal group for specific information and follow up.

The business leader or manager should own the role and stand by the attributes, skills and competencies set forth and drive all interviews and candidate sourcing to those requirements and preferences. This will ensure a non-biased and fair process. Overall, there are many KPIs used in measuring talent acquisition success. From the recruiter's point of view, the volume of interest, quality of candidate, complexity of the role, time to fill, diversity of pool, candidate experience etc., are all key indicators of their personal involvement. The hiring manager wants the best candidate, at the best price for an expected length of time and no excess baggage coming into their business.

Other tools that help to expedite and keep the process on track include social recruitment techniques and sourcing. Today the recruitment process is nearly all done on line. Filling the Roster includes the public marketing of a job all the way through on boarding, including the government paperwork and other orientation pieces. The internet helps expedite and organize the process and allows for better reporting and archiving records.

Supply and Demand

There are programs designed to supply the professional entry or advanced levels. They include internships, where college students gain experience in your company, under the supervision of managers and staff who should take that responsibility seriously and help it lead to future hires. That helps mitigate risk of hires, knowing someone's track record through personal experience is a big factor.

A Co-Op is another program, usually through a college that allows for a full semester of work/study, again designed to be a perfect fit for the next professional assignment. The Co-Op role is similar to an internship, whereby the Co-Op is usually a paid full time role and perhaps a business agreement between the business and school is in place to create the environment in which to train. Credit is attained with a professional evaluation from the business leadership.

Referrals come from all areas of the business community, inside and outside of an organization. There should be scrutiny placed on these as employees typically refer those they feel could do the job and handle the responsibilities. Often employees or their friends may refer family and friends and that may lead down the wrong path if left unsupervised as a program. Many executives may refer people who they may be related to, in family or through business contacts, and as a courtesy to the candidate, they may mandate an interview or even a role to hire them in. Be careful and discreet when accepting referrals to gauge who they came from and how to professionally reach out and guide the candidate through the job navigation process. Make sure you are clear on what, if any expectations, there are when accepting any referral for a job.

Rotational programs are very good in determining the right fit for the candidate going through. They might get a six or even twelve month assignment in one or more areas of business before a decision is made to place them permanently. They are usually post graduate degree candidates or entry level professionals. Some companies rely on this for their future leaders and management pool of candidates. Each of these programs requires organizing, diligence, tough selections and a commitment in the management and workforce to execute.

There are many other ways to find employees and great future leaders for your company. Sometimes the roles are easy to source, plenty of talent in the pool and others may be so specialized that companies must outsource the role of sourcing to critically and experienced contractors. In any case, the more care and attention you play in the process of filling your roster, the more successful you and your business will be. Think of each occurrence that creates a vacancy as an opportunity to excel and push the business forward.

CHAPTER 7
Your Workforce Reflects Your Business

Diversity is a significant term in today's workplace and amongst the workforce. Enriching the environment where we convene our business each day is an important step in human relationships and an essentially good cultural and societal practice. It emboldens the workforce to accept and include everyone, two very important traits in a bristling and often cold business climate. A great environment and company culture also transcends into the marketplace.

Diversity of Thought

The components of enrichment are varied. Let's examine diversity of thought. Differences can spur great conversation, debate, collaboration and ultimately resolution, which are all great attributes of a successful business environment. For example, diversity of thought allows multiple opinions and opportunities from various parties that offer recommendations in the decision-making process. This should lead to good results, having weighed the pros and cons, and reach sound conclusions. Diversity of thought is not meant to create confusion and dissension. Rather, conflict fosters disparate points of view and in the cultural acceptance of opinion, should steer towards resolution. The expression "agree to disagree" is true after discussing options and resolving issues, likely with compromise. In some cases, it's important to reach a settlement and move on, even when it's agreed upon that a resolution is worth more than moving forward without one.

Diversity of thought can also be managed and used as a productive tool. Often decisions are made in business that consider many options before rolling out. No one single answer can fit all scenarios and satisfy all parties each time. Manage diversity of thought closely and allow workforce and leaders alike to contribute, debate responsibly (and respectfully) and you'll see an engaged workforce. An engaged workforce will lead to a productive and culturally balanced workplace. That also strengthens and enriches a workforce.

Culture can play an important part of any successful business. Many top business leaders endorse an enriched culture in the workplace and workforce. Culture is an important foundation to help fortify their plans to better serve in the community or industry. A good company culture will be defined by many things, especially by the people who work inside. Many businesses are made up of a collection of employees who reflect the community they work in or the consumer base they connect with. They are the embodiment of a company and not only those who serve as the public facing ambassadors, especially those who directly interface in sales, marketing, retail, hospitality, public service, and so on. All workforce should feel connected to each other and the company brand. How you bring them together and how they interact with each other and your vendors and consumers is very important for your business to succeed.

Success is not only measured by the bottom line. A key indicator of success is attributed to the way a workforce is valued in their own company.

How you set them up for growth, development, community interaction (internal or external communities), and how comfortable they are in expressing themselves and participating in the company business will be factored into the overall melding of workforce and workplace. That will be an equation that resolves a value proposition for the workforce. Success often is a direct reflection company culture.

The management and workforce can each impact, both positively and negatively, the culture of the workplace. It's human nature to work in an inclusive environment, though the competition for total rewards (assignments, promotions, pay raises, bonuses, etc.) may be palpably competitive. That should not diminish from respecting each other and delivering good service, to the customers, vendors and co-workers. The workplace should be a friendly and inviting environment. A blend of people, process and safe/secure systems should be a good start.

Diversity of Background

Where does our enrichment physically start? A simple answer is everywhere. America is a country of immigrants, 240 years and counting. The settlers from all parts of the world came here and created families and communities that continue to evolve. Geography is a great differentiator to supply us with diverse thoughts, customs and business sense. For example, there is no doubt how culture is different in the urban centers of the megalopolis, (from Boston to Washington DC), versus the deeper southeast, Midwest, southern California or northwest cities. Each area of our country brings incredible opportunities to share backgrounds, ideas and of course, solutions.

Diversity also helps our nationally recognized brands to have a positive impact in the communities they sell to. The workforce is made up of people who have settled in our communities, moved about, been educated throughout the country and have gone to work at various companies. Think of how rich an internal culture is when people from all corners, colors and faiths come together and all work together on a unified direction for the same company.

How would a company implement such enriching strategies? The combined staff and management engagement is an essential catalyst. There must be a concerted level of acceptance and that may get roots from the contributions of each level of the workforce. All staff will have ideas and firsthand knowledge of what works and what doesn't. Enrichment training begins with discussion, an open and honest conversation where there are no wrong answers, just a respectful and no holes-barred dialogue. If all the elements of current state are open for discussion, pull out the easy wins and figure them out first. Once there are solutions that are collaborative and agreed on, tackle some of the tougher situations, these may require a multilevel approach whereby management and staff work together on the initiatives. Have an impartial leader who can steer the conversations respectfully towards solutions and not arguments or finger pointing. Sometimes training strategies and implementation in the enriching of a workforce and workplace takes time and refinements.

Training your Workforce

Often, thorough diversity training starts with an open forum where the meeting is a conversation, talking about the aspects of enrichment that are expected to have a positive and forward thinking impact on business and staff alike. Once the conversation is out in the open and feedback is considered, start to focus and filter the next steps as a direct response to the workforce. There are various ways to implement enrichment programs, just know that you must understand what is going to work in your business, listen to the groups and offer the programs with their help. Engagement is a key indicator of interest and ultimately a measurement of success.

There are many options from which to organize and refine enrichment programs for your business. Once the leaders agree on implementation, do some research on where to find support or shared best practices from outside organizations. A web search on diversity in the workplace will reveal plenty of options, so your duty should be to read up and choose some of the options that align with your business mission and values. There are top organizations who offer many ways to support enrichment. Outreach to such key leaders and organizations is critical. Choose from the best available resources that come from consulting groups or organizations that offer services, programs and support to diversity or enrichment.

Your workforce need not think of implementing enrichment programs as re-inventing the wheel. There are many tried and true programs to employ and emulate. Think of diversity as a necessary part of your value proposition. Diversity as a value includes so many options to consider, including your everyday messaging, creating a safe and welcoming workplace environment, product and services manufacturing and distribution, sales, marketing and most especially, talent acquisition.

Focus on Inclusion

Developing good process, protocol and workforce development should include a focus on inclusion. This is an important component to understand. The term diversity refers to different or disparate elements. In many business opportunities, diversity brings thought, people, points of view and so many other factors to a setting. Inclusion is the process of blending. In business, inclusion may refer to the integration of the diverse elements presented for consideration towards resolution. Typically, diversity refers to numbers on a roster, a reflection of the workforce by their gender or cultural origins. This is only one component, which is very sensitive, and too often looked at with critical scrutiny. It's very important to blend or integrate as many different points of view into any problem-solving situation to get the most balanced, fair and equitable result. Inclusion allows for many parties to input and all to agree. That's a good ideal to reach for.

Another key component of diversity and enrichment deals with vendors and business relationships, known as Supplier Diversity. Simply, who are you doing business with? How are your vendors representing themselves? Your workforce and your workplace will be impacted positively by good Supplier Diversity. There are support groups and organizations who help suppliers to balance themselves in a similar way, hiring and growing staff appropriately that reflect their own business. They also create a positive workplace and have a diverse management team, often led by minority owners. Your customers and clients will assess your overall relationship at times of decision making and will consider your Supplier Diversity as a component to measure. When a business is faced with making choices, sometimes the best decisions for the greater good will start with enriching the culture and offering a well-intentioned and balanced approach to all

Workforce and Workplace

Simply, the workforce is your employed staff, no matter their status, and their workplace is a work station or base, a physical space, perhaps a home office, a mobile office, etc. The workplace is a destination for a collection of workers, vendors, consumers and/or contractors to collaborate skills and execute strategies that become shared experiences and all expect to succeed in.

The actual diversity of the workforce can be measured through demographics, meaning the workforce will be broken down into several ways to build data streams, such as how many, from where and at what level are they employed. Gender, ethnicity and other factors are generally self-identified by the workforce themselves and that information is aggregated into HR systems. There are laws and other regulations that stipulate the privacy and protection of personal identity and your HR systems are the place to house the data and protect the company. As such, many business leaders may not know their true diversity demographics, so it is imperative to have the conversation with the leadership, ownership, or partner in HR, to understand any obligation towards a balanced and strategically diverse workforce.

Strategic recruitment may identify gaps or direction for a business to acquire new workforce and talent. The responsibility and accountability may be beyond the reach of the line managers, though they should have a good understanding of the company mission and how recruitment fits. One very important aspect of workforce development is managing feeder programs. Feeder programs can be the best asset a manager could hope for. They are generally comprised of students, interns, apprentice types. These programs are typically low cost and many develop young talent quickly into the roles they can fit into in the various businesses, which is economically effective, especially at the right price. Many companies work directly with schools to cultivate a learning program from which to surface great candidates and impact both organizations. Managers need to embrace these programs, create an environment to educate and motivate the students and take advantage of the opportunity to train them while they are still enrolled in school. They can recoup that investment in training some months later when the interns graduate or bring them back for another term.

Other feeder programs could include or be part of returning military veterans, trade organizations and contingent staffing agencies. Your business can find opportunities to expand cultural bounds by looking at all options, where applicable, to recruiting and staffing.

Many industries have trade organizations that support the products, people, process and history of the trades they work within. Most trades will also have ethnic, niche or other classification of collections of workers. Examples of these trade organizations includes NABJ (National Association of Black Journalists) for media and SHPE (Society of Hispanic Professional Engineers) for a cross section of engineering, math and computer science. Still other groups such as LGBT supported organizations are groups that help ensure fair and equitable business practices, especially in recruiting, supplier diversity and promotional advancement opportunities.

The reason to stress the organizational support is applicable to all areas in HR, that each has industry support and history to call on for best practices and shared services. There are great thought leaders, practitioners, consultants and inspirational professionals who continue to advance the learning, craft, profile and value of human resources trades. Knowing some of what the HR partners can offer to your workforce or workplace should both inspire and motivate you to take advantage of that relationship or opportunity in any way to further your company or division.

In the workplace, disparate groups can work together. These include differences by geography, race, creed and other factors such as parental, generational and so on. Many companies have formed affinity groups whereby these groups of people in the workforce can come together in off hours and share stories, cultures and other interactions. Some groups help enrichment by bringing in speakers, others volunteer in the community and still others may go out to a social event like a ballgame or bowling. These are also known as employee resource groups, supporting each other through common themes. The workplace is enriched greatly when employees get together and share themselves. Inclusion is a powerful tool for managers to align with. In some advanced cases, the affinity groups also allow friends or allies to join the groups and that helps to share experiences. This helps spread messages, share cultures and become valuable to business in recruitment or even reflecting the customer base. Business resource and affinity groups can produce great results in advancing company culture.

The bottom line on enriching a workforce and workplace is to hire a diverse enough staff to reflect the customer base and engage them in helping shape a friendly and inclusive place to work. Keep it safe and free of harassment, ensuring all who work or otherwise interact in the workplace feel safe and secure. Create a place where the workforce feel they can own a piece of it, keep it orderly and clean. The wellness of the staff is also very important and anything an owner or manager can do to foster healthy conditions is also a sign of an enriched and inclusive workplace.

Business Advocacy

CHAPTER 8
Who's Got Your Back?

I n the simplest terms, every business needs an advocate. An advocate will be the personal and professional partner for all things to run smoothly, a dispatcher, a legal adviser, traffic coordinator, calendar creator and advisor all rolled into one. In many cases, a business owner or manager may not have the luxury of retaining an advocate and will incorporate these roles under their own hat. In HR, the professionals stress the value of business acumen. Let's explore how these traits help support your business.

Business generally runs on a cyclical calendar. Finance, accounting, quarterly reports, purchasing, holidays, etc. all contribute to the forecasting and reviewing of business. Long range planning takes annual increments of time. Planning for a business can be put into a calendar format, no matter when the fiscal, performance and/or sales years start and finish because they will all divide by twelve months. Know your annual events. Your partner or advocate will support this.

Consultant and Adviser

A Business Advocate is the equivalent of the HR Business Partner or in the past would be an HR Generalist. The Generalist or Partner is not always a specialized professional, such as a recruiter, compensation, training or diversity leader. They are akin to a general physician, someone who can assess broad areas and help to make the early decisions by bringing in key decision-making criteria, support business teams or objectives and make recommendations to keep the flow moving. The Advocate supports the business workflow events as well as workforce management annual details. They consult a business and management team through the various calendar and the cross over events. This is part of having a business acumen and offering valued perspective.

Planning for events will incorporate a great deal of project managing, for example an annual holiday sale starts months ahead in the surveying, marketing, purchasing, pricing, scheduling, shipping, receiving, stocking and rehearsal phases. These all take place before the actual sales event. Add to this list planning for resources, posting jobs, hiring, on boarding, training, performance managing, etc. and you start to get an idea of how the annual business calendar of events can be critically important to your success. Managing the workforce also includes strategic events in performance, training, organizational development, etc. Your role as a manager should include some component of business management and/or advocacy. Some companies assign these roles to HR Generalists or Business Partners, who are assigned to specific divisions and help to navigate the business carousel. In many others, managers share these responsibilities.

A manager or a business owner, who also acts as the advocate, may find efficiencies with respect to the calendar, depending upon the company or business. Knowing all the varied roles and responsibilities available to be a good advocate, the leader or manager can make decisions to outsource, offload or delegate certain event planning of the calendar to trusted staff or vendors to help fill in the gaps. It's important to know what's going well in addition to what's missing in the advocacy role. Think of the role as being a consultant of all things business. The advocate can prompt the business leaders throughout the event cycles, keeping them abreast of timelines.

A trusted Business Advocate is welcomed and considered a valuable resource for any business owner, leader or manager. This adviser consults on any number of business decisions and projects, making sure the business leaders remember to consider all factors, data and information available when making decisions, whether those resolutions relate to people or process. This centralized role helps to widen vision and mitigate legal risk when properly accepted and integrated into the business planning. That point should be reinforced. The Advocate or HR Partner is there to protect the business in most decisions, both as a consultant (competent and cost effective business flow) and adviser (legal or compliance guide).

The business management team is typically more experienced and specialized in their specific industry and throughput, and still the collaboration with a trusted Advocate is essential. If the Advocate is a separate team member or HR professional, it requires on-going communication and trust between them so all parties understand, respect and allow each other to contribute, conflict when necessary and solve issues. If the business leader also serves as their own Advocate, it's imperative to have the training and experience required to make thorough and accurate decisions and have considered all available information leading up to resolution. Consider your role in the business as a manager and what responsibility you have in problem solving or annual business flow.

Transparency

A great contribution that a Business Advocate shares is information. Communicating at all levels is important and critical for the Advocate to be aware of the volume, cadence and discretion of any information that will be shared with management and the workforce. Therefore, it is important to regulate the information flow whether the role of the Advocate is outsourced, internal, shared or otherwise owned by a business leader.

One benefit of having a Business Advocate or an HR Partner working with you is facilitating communication with employees at all levels. These leaders can share information appropriately and quite often are regarded as a voice of reason. Many employees surface ideas or workflow recommendations, for example, and a good advocate can help them to understand the cost, discuss the necessary resources or the prohibitive aspects of the idea. Remember that they are trained to communicate appropriately on a variety of topics and situations. They help set realistic expectations. A key aspect of the advocate role is to be approachable and direct with feedback.

A Business Advocate measures communication carefully, usually to protect or preserve discretionary information. A successful business will share just enough information to allow all workforce, including management and senior leaders to have the correct information to deal internally or externally on business or even social communication. Generally, the higher up a role in a company the more likely they will be in social circles or conferences where even the most casual conversations may be overheard and often misinterpreted. The more experienced one becomes in leading, managing or otherwise advocating on behalf of business, the tighter the control of information and conversation. Leaders are often the ones most quoted.

People will hear and receive messages differently from peers and other members of the workforce, so it's very important to state and restate policy changes and company information. A good rule of thumb is to also send out follow up information in written form to reinforce and break through any barriers in the original communication. Remember, the more you diversify the workforce, usually to reflect your customer base and enrich our workplace, the more you need to consider the many types of culture and comprehension of how you announce or implement changes. Everyone may receive communication differently, so it's imperative to have written statements to back up any announcements in organizational or policy changes. Business Advocates are equipped to oversee the typical and strategic communications.

Sharing information is important and there are many factors to consider beforehand. Who will listen to you and how will they receive and absorb the message, whether written or spoken? How will you react to positive and/or negative responses? These are reasonable scenarios you should consider, at the very least, before sharing information on a large scale, such as to a workforce. No matter the nature of the message, there will always be differences of opinion and points of view. You should be prepared to deliver information in a way that will mitigate the most controversial "public" responses and be able to deal with the typical ones in a professional and timely manner.

It's important to note that advocating for a business will not always be regarding positive news. It may be critically important information at times and must always be factual, accurate and defensible. The Business Advocate must be adept at speaking, writing and listening in a professional style. Policy changes are often delivered within the context of a business or corporate communication to the workforce. Policies have multiple interpretations and often disparate groups will hear and receive differently. Individuals will read or listen carefully and draw first impressions. If they are not aligned to the speaker, a conflict, argument or standoff may ensue.

Being prepared for each eventuality will make the business of communication and business advocacy more effective.

Let's consider two types of information flow. The first type is cascading the message. Cascading information is a normal protocol and deals with information traveling "downhill". This is typically the information that either starts with or gets reinforced at a management level and sent down to the workforce. It's an incredibly effective tool when done correctly.

Let's create a scenario which involves a corporate or senior level communication coming out and needs a quick acceptance and implementation. An example would be a policy change that may require some in the workforce to alter schedules or personally change something in their daily routines to enact the new policy. While this may seem to be somewhat benign, there will likely be some in the workforce who feel they didn't have a voice in the new change and think the senior leadership is out of touch with them. Perhaps the organization is large enough that the origin of the communication may be several corporate levels above the workforce where the communication is headed. Due to the nature of the org structure, it is likely that there are several levels of connecting and passing information in a timely manner. This now may need intermediary steps in endorsing the information. To mitigate a negative initial reaction, which is very common, senior leaders can preempt the announcement with a memo to their middle or line managers who can send down or "cascade" the information to their workforce with their personal endorsements. This shows continuity amongst the management tier. The middle managers may end up asking anyone with questions to see them directly and support their workforce right to communicate. That sends a message to the workforce that they are important enough to consider ahead of the general announcement and that their own managers had their voice throughout the process. This is a good practice way of extending communications and offering open dialogue.

In contrast, the workforce may have the opportunities to send ideas and recommendations for changes up to the senior leadership. That flow of information is important to manage and if done well, can help great communication in a bi-directional way. This is known as escalating communication. It's important for the workforce to know they can send thoughts and/or responses to their managers and senior leaders in a professional manner, without consequences. The escalation of ideas may start as a conduit, and end up being filtered. The Business Advocate can help the workforce understand the best practices of sending information up to senior levels and how to expedite the process. Typically, this is a slower form of communication, as each level is pitching or advocating for the message to continue to the next level and beyond, if necessary, to enact changes. By contrast, when a decision is made at the higher levels, it is expected that the flow down will be efficient and effectively timely. Still, a business that allows and encourages communicating ideas upward for approval, is likely a strong organization, that feels secure in its empowerment of the workforce. At each stage, there should be just enough substance, clarity and efficiency of the message to meet the expectations at higher levels of management.

There is no certainty that the communication will ultimately be approved or induce change, though it does foster a true sense of support for the workforce in exercising their voice. If the workforce understands these best practices and the opportunity to be heard, they can decide how to approach it to suit their needs. This is a good way of training them for future roles and ensuring good culture.

Ultimate Advocacy

Earlier in Chapter 4, Employee Advocacy, we noted some critical responsibilities regarding Workplace Incidents, specifically harassment claims and workplace violence threats. Whether you are advocating on behalf of the workforce or workplace, it's important to meld these roles.

Business Advocates are generally good at project or program management. Each of these roles requires specific communication and timely milestones. In project or program management, communication is a key function. Some of the communication that needs to be filtered and appropriately managed by a Business Advocate or HR Partner could deal with workforce development and succession planning. Quite simply, workforce development deals with moving pieces and, at times, adding and/or deleting company resources, including the workforce itself. Succession planning deals with those in the organization who are the up and coming stars. They are being pointed out, touted by managers and senior leaders for future opportunities based upon their current rise in performance and responsibilities. These are very discretionary exercises and important to the business and bottom line. Managers need to assess performance and rate or rank their assigned employees with respect to personal goals and business objectives. They should work hand in hand with their HR partner or, in some cases, take that responsibility on themselves.

Communication is such an important competency to Advocates and managers alike. Not all conversations with your employees are positive, in fact, about half are tough to prepare for and deliver. These may include performance management discussions, disciplinary hearings and dismissals. Each of these examples sets a stage for conflict, argument, negotiation, confusion and disagreement. The Business Advocates are trained to help mitigate emotional and stressful conversations and keep dialogue as professional and balanced as possible. Not all conversations will go successfully, so beware of your role as a manager and what part you play in the communication of resolution or assessment. The briefest and most straightforward method of communication is usually the most effective. So many conversations in these types of settings are explosive by nature, so the least said is considered the best course. It may not sit well with you in your personal feelings for someone but is certainly part of the role as a manager.

Any misinterpretation or misjudgment could be detrimental, especially when the public is informed through social media or other means. A Business Advocate, often an HR professional, should be trained and experienced in filtering communication, steering the flow and offering well thought out plans. The communication of these initiatives is important to manage appropriately. The advocate role should be both a supporter and devil's advocate at the same time. They should point out process and industry standards to those involved in the decision making or those in the workforce and on the receiving end of decisions. Advocates also help a business to put the right specialists on projects that require planning, implementation, change management, execution and sustainment. These are terms that all good projects will go through. The advocate role should help to find the right expertise, bring in case studies and allow for discussion, deliberation and resolution. That's good work for a Business Advocate.

The Business Advocate is a conduit for all types of workflow, project and change management, business calendar and compliance management, performance management, business process, communication and more. They typically work between the business unit and the governing body, whether it be a senior leader group or an HR division. They should be able to interpret each side and communicate effectively. As leaders, the

Business Advocate supports and endorses development of business, workforce, workplace and future leaders. They help to analyze projects and business objectives to offer recommendations for best industry practices, legal compliance and overall scope of business workflow. In the absence of an internal HR division, managers should assume as much of the business role and responsibility and advocate appropriately. When it comes to business support, the Business Advocate has your back.

CHAPTER 9

The Cream Will Rise in Business

Management is a special term. Simply, the word implies control, organization and administration. Business can pass or fail based on the performance of management. There are many variations of management, identified by title, direct responsibility and areas of oversight. Often, managers may oversee multiple teams or divisions. At times, managers or business owners may wear several hats, still in big corporations, managers might lead single areas, based on their specialized background and expertise. In all cases, best practices of management should be expected, encouraged and measured for performance and success. What management does not automatically infer is leadership. That is a special competency bundle we will cover.

Whether you own or manage a sandwich shop, a boutique store, a large firm or corporation, as a manager, you may be responsible for multiple roles. When you manage a workforce, you are responsible for people. That means their livelihoods, their inspirations, aspirations and platforms for financial or learned success can be tied directly to you and your oversight. The workforce looks to managers and senior leaders as not only decision makers but ultimately gatekeepers. How your employees advance in the business may be up to your recommendations. Your decisions can affect the workforce in many ways and always directly with respect to rewards and advancement. Managers at times yield a powerfully significant role. When it involves people, power is a very sensitive tool and the best managers lead with balance and discretionary skills.

Motivation is a special trait that the best managers have. It is an "it" factor in having a well-run operation. Managers who build good teams and exceed expectations usually motivate their workforce in various ways. Motivation for an employee is important as they need to show up and give their all to make the business run well. Do they perform well because of you, their manager? What makes them excited or proud to be part of your team may result in better performance or higher standards. All the puzzle pieces fit best when motivation is driving the workforce. It is a competency that managers and leaders exude.

Something attracts us to certain roles and companies. The motivation to work may be money, benefits or some combination that helps us in survival. Then there are companies and special individuals who find ways to create an environment that is special to be a part of and makes working there seem pleasurable and inviting. Is that the type of manager you are or one you'd like to become? What would it take to lead with skills and competencies that inspire and motivate your workforce to produce even better results? Think of some great leaders, coaches, teachers, etc. What set them apart and how did they inspire or motivate others? Special leaders have extraordinary abilities to get the most out of their followers and workforces. Managers should know that they are looked at closely by their workforce and their traits and characteristics are often imitated and especially when they are successful.

Process, Projects, Programs, People

Let's examine some of the aspects of managing and contrast those job responsibilities to what leadership requires. Perhaps you manage a supply chain or a workflow, such as a manufacturing process. Or you may manage products, services, logistics and vendors. The list can be boundless. Let's look closely at basic management, which is commonly done in a linear fashion, for example, someone managing one or more people or process in a similar line of business. Linear managing is basic at its core. It follows the simple direction of organizational work flow, where roles and responsibilities flow from bottom to top on a chart and conversely is managed from top to bottom.

As manager, you may be required to fully understand the concepts, the technologies, the processes, the handoffs, the interactions with suppliers, the sales agreements, the service level agreements, the shipping and handling process, etc. You can start to see where a manager needs a comprehensive knowledge of all the points in the life cycle of a product, process or program to be well rounded. If a manager is overseeing people and therefore responsible for their performance, growth and output, he/she can add many additional soft skills and competencies to their personal agenda. These competencies include working with people, communication techniques, goal setting, performance management and more. The better the skills, the better the chances that as managers go, the cream will rise to the top.

Managing in a linear fashion is important, can be intricate and intense. Managing one person and one process will test you as a new manager and when you add more workforce and multiple programs, process and projects, you can see where the evolution of growth to a seasoned manager is so important. Early on, managers need to learn as much about the basic requirements and expectations, absorb best practices and implement good strategies. Personal growth in management can be exponential.

Many organizations are interdependent with others and some merge business units or centralized services across geographies, divisions and companies. Take an example of a franchised fast food restaurant. Corporate policies and branding may happen in a centralized and powerfully funded way, though the core business is locally owned, operated and managed. This is all part of the matrix style of business. It's not a *do it yourself* business as the complete support for all systems and services is strictly managed by the corporate sector. That's where the brand is also managed. Still, it's the opportunity to source, hire and manage people who operate under tried and true workflow. If you are a manager in this type of company, your opportunities to affect change may be limited or restricted, based on the corporate structure of communication, and your personal advancement may be best to approach horizontally, to other local franchises, who may need your specific experience and you can find opportunities to rise and help grow these smaller entities. Once you attain a certain level locally, more regional or geographical opportunities start to surface and so on. Be aware of your corporate opportunities as those roles may suit you or you workforce rising stars at times.

Mergers and acquisitions in today's world are common place and may result in collaborative management, hybrid teams and new work flows. Managing in that environment can be complicated. Learn how your business works and where decisions are made. How influential are the decision makers as you go up the organizational chart? Where does the culture shift, where do the roles become across divisions or companies and so on? It's more complex to manage in a matrix organization because there may be merging lines of business, cultures, rules and benefits.

Managers must be aware of other divisions and business units that are not directly associated with them so they can understand how to cascade or escalate communication, how to deal with a hybrid HR division and how to ultimately affect the bottom line and grow the company from their own role and team. Staying aware of changing rules and how business information and communication flows are very important as you manage in a matrix organization.

A good manager should be self-motivated to upgrade their soft skills and competencies. Learn what drives your company's mission, its business and the culture. Try to strengthen the skills and influence some of that drive and make yourself a better and more impactful manager. For example, if your company culture is devoted to growing and supporting diversity, you, as a manager should learn how to source for the best candidates, educate the best talent on your team and infuse an inclusive environment. Make yourself a better manager by paying attention to the details of competencies related to your role, your division and your company.

Project management is an essential tool in any manager's portfolio. There are various types of project management styles and it's important to understand the basic structure of PM so line managers can be responsible and accountable when assigned to contribute to projects. Business relies heavily on planned and carefully executed projects that improve productivity in many areas and while we won't go into any specifically, it's important to know how to react and respond to PM. Some managers may dispatch members of their workforce to cross-division projects and it's also imperative that they get the full support and resources to successfully contribute to the overall project. This shouldn't be taken lightly because any projects approved by senior levels should be considered as priority and those managing projects should be identified as leaders. Managers should be prepared to make changes and adapt to conditional circumstances especially when their resources may be impacted. Good analytical skills and a wherewithal of how the business unit works will foster growth and development in a manager.

Similarly, a good manager or business leader must be organized with respect to the people under their direct and indirect supervision. Who they are is critical to know, where they came from and how they got to this point in time is very important to consider when setting them up for your expectations, creating individual goals or assessing strengths and weaknesses in general assignment, succession or promotional planning.

An example of good organizational detail for you on behalf of your workforce would be to create a baseball card for your individual employees. A baseball card has the picture, name and basic description of a player, with position and team. On the reverse side, it's crammed with statistics and history of professional employment, education, other important facts. Isn't that what a resume looks like? Think of how easy it is to carry a card, identify a player and quickly understand the journey to get to their team. Now, put that same process into effect on your team and in your workforce. A good manager will be able to see staff member, be refreshed on their background and understand the current state better.

How often do you touch base, have a conversation or plan work initiatives with anyone or everyone in your direct workforce? How much of their individual input is solicited, considered, valued and/or rewarded? An engaged workforce stays motivated and focused. They will work hard and do better for an approachable and sincere manager. An engaged workforce stays driven to succeed for their manager and their company.

Organizational Skills

Organizational skills can often spur creatively generated programs to help managers succeed. The term organization has multiple meanings. For example, according to *Merriam-Webster*, as a noun, organization means a collection of people with a particular purpose, such as a business, society or association. As an action, organization means orderly storing of things so they can be found easily, planning or arranging parts of an activity or process effectively. Whether structure or action, competent use of organization is essential to successfully managing.

Organization is a hallmark of strong management. It encompasses so much of the knowledge base and practical applications. For example, under knowledge base, a manager is stronger when he/she understands where things are (current state of the business or supply chain, as well how the business connects). Knowing the players, the workforce, the vendors, especially the marketplace and the competition will give a manager leverage. Why is leverage a key component? The short answer is that it allows managers to utilize experience and intelligence efficiently and operate with a wider view. Keeping the knowledge base within reach, updated and ready to support decisions and business flow, is part of the organizational theory.

Let's take a common occurrence as an example of knowledge as leverage in a business setting. Example, you as manager will be scheduled to meet with a strategic vendor, one your firm has a long-standing relationship with and you will be meeting in person. Meeting with a strategic vendor in person is an old school but still relevant communication tool and may be an important step to new or future collaboration. How much do you or your business leaders really know about the history of business with this vendor or firm, the former (or current) state of the relationship, any outstanding issues or finances, etc.? These small points are important to consider in keeping a business to business relationship effective. Having a history to recall how your relationship evolved, knowing what is currently on the books for each of your points of view and where the industry may be headed are so important to the present conversation and potentially new ground to cover together. This is a process that relies on a strong Customer (Client) Management System (CMS) tool. Use this type of relationship management in many instances of business. Invest in good organizational skills and you will leverage solid leadership qualities.

Reporting and Planning

An important piece of managing is knowing how and when to file a report. Many business leaders will rely on their managers to report, especially from divisions such as production, operations or sales when the leaders are not present. What should all managers do to prepare for basic reporting? The first thing managers should do is to be clear on the business leaders' expectations for your reporting. Are there templated styles to follow or will your reports be free form and opinionated? There are many types of reports, from travel and expense, to sales, project status, operational and so on. Always ask questions for clarity of the expected information, cadence and follow up strategies. Know whom to send the reports and where they may end up, to appropriately address and sign off on the information within. Remember that in today's immediate networking age, your written or published report, in any form or state of construction, may end up in any number of unforeseen locations, including lower staff levels and the office of the CEO. The information flow is faster than ever and you may never get a chance to recall it. Be careful, own it and be honest. Organization, with respect to reporting, is a key component.

Another aspect of managing is short and long term planning. Planning is an important business step to keep the operations running smoothly and without disruption. A manager should know what the tools and resources are, where they are located, how far along the life cycle, how to replenish them and how to sharpen them for future technologies and workflow. Keep the trains running on the tracks and on time. That's the simple answer. Start with supplies necessary to do the job (e.g. office essentials, networking components, furniture, etc.) and manage the recycling efforts. The higher you rise in management, the likelihood of deeper and longer range planning you are expected to produce. This includes decisions buoyed by future technological solutions, targeted research and education on your part to stay relevant to your company and industry. Long range planning may come along with prioritization and budgeting techniques, profit and loss (P & L) statements, forecasting headcount and more. The various types of planning and reporting are very much tied to roles, companies, industries that each have variant expectations.

Soft Skills

Managing takes a certain level of skill, commitment and patience. It also takes training, experience and time to be comfortable and successful at it. Managing people successfully requires all of this and more. There is a physical and a psychological science to managing people well enough to also be considered a leader. The term leader may be in your job title or job description. Overseeing business or any part of it comes with expectations of leadership. If managing is aligned with organization, then leading is akin to inspiration.

Leadership is critical in any company or industry to survive and/or thrive. Leadership is very much a soft skill. Many words can describe the various parts of leadership, such as motivational, inspirational, integrity, stimulating, honest, genuine, etc. Leadership originates within a person and is reflected in their style. Managers who are also leaders carry themselves a bit differently and offer support, encouragement and feedback appropriately. They don't go overboard with praise or criticism and stay balanced in judgment and resolution. Leaders are selfless and often work on behalf of the greater good. Leaders are not always popular with everyone, based on the decisions they are responsible to make. They often think wider and more fairly than average managers.

Decision making is one of the most essential parts of managing and leadership. How a decision is made, steps towards a conclusion, moving forward through change management and executing a new direction are parts of a leader's role. A major part of business is communication and how a leader communicates can push a business to success. Managing through the process of workforce activities, the annual calendar of events and one on one conversations is simply not enough to stay ahead in business. These are expected processes to manage and a good leader will add intangible and demonstrable qualities that stand above.

Take performance management for example. Going through the paces of setting goals and reviewing performance annually is not enough to motivate the workforce to push themselves to get better at their craft and make themselves and/or the company more valuable. A leader will meet more frequently and engage employees on how they are doing and how they can continue to grow and evolve in their roles. A leader will stretch individuals' goals and open wide the horizon for the workforce to consider for educating or informing themselves. A leader utilizes feedback from the workforce to better him/herself and reinforces how valuable the workforce is when they participate in the exercise. Managers learn early how performance management is important to any business success. Managers work with the workforce to benchmark where individuals are versus company objectives, peers and external threats. Leaders will find a way to focus on top performers, where applicable, and get the most out of them. On-going conversation throughout the performance year allows for adjustments and modifications to existing goals so a business truly has a track record of its workforce. That's good leadership skill on display.

Communicating with Style

Leaders handle conflict resolution appropriately. Every conversation or decision has various points of view and when it comes to resolution, the workforce and management don't always see eye to eye. A good leader listens and considers multiple points of view before handing down decisions where conflict arose. Conflict, when treated with respect, offers diversity of thought and engages parties to respectfully offer collaboration, compromise and resolutions. Leaders are important to the overall communication process and skilled in motivating the workforce.

An important piece of leadership is having a good understanding of how you, as a leader, are perceived by others. How you speak, how you write and even your non-verbal communication, (e.g. how you conduct yourself in group settings and social forums) are key indicators of your emotional intelligence or emotional quotient. People receive your messages in a variety of ways and will spark an emotional response, whether positive or negative, to you. This also has an impact on how others absorb, believe or react to your communication. It's best to stay as balanced and/or genuine as possible in the social settings, first impression meetings and when communicating company business or policy. This will help your workforce garner trust and support for you. Emotional Intelligence is a key feedback indicator of your reception amongst the workforce, if not your popularity. Not all businesses are alike and communication can be vastly different so understanding your Emotional Intelligence is important.

Discussing future opportunities with your employees is a very sensitive and personal component of leadership and critical to yours and your business success. This role involves facilitating effective career conversations. The workforce is generally more worried or nervous when talking about themselves than the manager or leader having that dialogue with them. These are typically awkward one on one discussions about an employee's career path and what they or you can do to impact it or sway them from a disastrous move. Often, managers may get "too corporate" and speak about job descriptions or try to dissuade someone or even threaten them not to state publicly about considering a move. Inexperienced managers tend to think of protecting the business and keeping the status quo regarding all employees they supervise. Every business is different and none have a "one size fits all" answer here.

As a leader, you should know your business, your horizontal divisions and companies. See and hear the conversation through the eyes and ears of your workforce. Be fair, direct and straight with them. If you don't have the power to affect a move, talk about how you got to where you are, the work, the study, the performance, whatever you think it was. Not every company will have a path for all employees, based on the industry and economics. A goof leader can talk about how employees can learn more while they are in their present role and become more valuable or marketable. If there is no apparent avenue for your workforce to grow beyond the current role, they will find advancement means stepping out and into another workplace and invest in themselves.

Motivate your workforce to step up and seek higher roles. It's okay to manage someone to a role higher than yours, good leaders make great leaders from their workforce at times. If you are inexperienced at the career conversation, motivate them to work hard, make those around them better and seek a meeting with your managers or senior leaders. Help to create the forum for them to speak about themselves to the decision makers and inspire them to continue to grow. Motivation is a great competency of leaders and a soft skill that is treasured. That's true leadership.

CHAPTER 10
What's Next?

Human Resources as a business community continues to evolve. The industry that supports business and corporate leaders is learning every day how to deliver programs and effective recommendations that keep companies compliant and on track. Gone are the days when the community was known as "Personnel". The connotation was meant to represent people. They had the locations, the resources and tools to support and maintain the workforce. With advancements in training and scope, the community of Human Resources is wider and more transferable than ever. They are considered to have true business acumen, advisers for your business leaders. Advocating for business and protecting company brand is now a major expectation of HR. Perhaps the next generation will simply refer to their HR support group as Advocacy. The Generalist became the Business Partner, not the Employee Partner. Perhaps that role should be divided again and I offer two solutions, Business Advocate and Employee Advocate. The latter should be more accessible and supportive on a regular basis. If that resource is unavailable in your business, the Manager role should rise to it.

Business owners, leadership and management also continue to evolve. The top managers are taking a record number of industries to the brink of technological and sociological heights. All the while there is still a gap between the myriad of institutions in industry and Human Resources to embrace, share and accept each other with collaborative expertise.

Shared Experiences

Managers in nearly every industry or company can learn from the HR skill sets as we've indicated throughout this book. Forget the historically, and at times rocky, relationships between industry management teams and the HR support. Whether insourced, outsourced or some combination or consultant style partnership, HR professionals are educated specifically to support the current or future state of business and keep them defensively protected from malpractice. The disciplines of HR are specialized and critically important to consider in nearly every decision made in a business objective. People, process, programs and projects are all covered equitably and with legal compliance to sensitive data in the HR disciplines. These specialized skill sets are necessary for the successful management of a business, whether HR is a present force or simply that the leaders take on all the roles and responsibilities of managing for themselves.

Another thought on the institutional claim of a rivalry between industry management and the HR community. Why is it that some business leaders and some HR professionals continue to hold this standoff? It may come down to human nature of command and control by those specially trained to lead. In business, the managers know the workflow, the process, skills, workflow, etc. and see the world through own experience and often through metrics of success. In HR, the professionals see their skill sets as honed, certified and well trained. They are closely aligned to a legal community. They should be doing business above board and within all regulatory parameters. The support they offer to any business unit should be with a goal of making a best decision and to advance the goals and ideals of the company, staying compliant regarding the use of the workforce and environmental state of the workplace. Both sides of business and HR partnership should understand, as best they can, the expectations and division of labor between themselves and agree to support each other's specialized roles. What often happens is a fight for control, even in a quiet way, which undermines the relationship. The goal of this book is to open the HR world to the managers of business so they can understand better and appreciate the education, training and mission of their HR team, or take that into account as they act alone.

In many cases, industry leaders simply cannot keep up with all the regulations and laws which govern workforce and workplace these days and should increase their understanding of their own HR responsibilities. Leaders should consider HR professionals as equal partners along with their own business teams. HR offers a bridge to legal and compliant decisions. They each need to overtly communicate their respect and acceptance of each other to their workforce.

Follow the Leader

It's a simple concept that we all experienced growing up. Follow the leader. Leadership is a special commodity and when you have the opportunity and good fortune to learn from a true leader, take advantage of that gift. Learn how leaders walk and talk when it comes to a variety of situations and circumstances. Leadership has a specialized bundle of soft skills and competencies. Managers and individual contributors can grow professionally by imitating, emulating and putting into practice the situational response techniques that leaders deliver.

Social media can be a double-edged sword at times. While the immediacy of distributing information and dispensation of messaging is extremely valuable, it is also incredibly fragile. We do not control electronic communications. Once out, emails and documents cannot be destroyed or permanently deleted. Therefore, any use of electronic media for communication is very sensitive. A manager at the early stage of a career or a seasoned CEO each must practice similar communication techniques. Managers should understand their roles in balancing words, speech and expectations as they practice sound techniques in communicating.

There are very experienced and successful leaders and leadership organizations available to teach you about this competency of communicating effectively. Many consulting and HR organizations, such as Society of Human Resources Management (SHRM), have a vast amount of information available to share with respect to the HR skills. Managers can find a lot of information, much of it free, to pursue continuing education in these disciplines. Leadership can find good information to share and help proliferate the success of business, based upon better and continuously improving managers.

Communicating is Key

Managers communicate in a variety of ways and means every day. They are put in positions of authority or leadership and how they act in social, community and business settings are just as important as the words they choose to set goals, report on situations or conditions and how they generally send out messages to the workforce. Managers may be held accountable for how, what and when they communicate inside and outside the business. The responsibility of managing may not always end at the door when you leave for the day. Knowing how you are perceived as well as received in communicating is an important step in the growth of a manager.

As covered earlier, managers routinely report on the state of business. Reporting to leaders and senior management is another part of critical and often sensitive communication. Information is an important commodity in business and the most effective way to use it will become the most valuable. Therefore, accuracy is imperative. Managers may not see their senior leaders every day or for long stretches. There could be several layers of management receiving your reports, that may end up in offices and screens you would never have intended. Perhaps an audit or court action is brought against your company and emails are subpoenaed. Your words and reports may now be held up as evidence or defensible in protection of your company. This may seem extreme, but is absolutely a reality in today's business climate. Take time to write, read and review your commentaries, reporting and any other type of communication in your business role.

Perhaps the most underrated form of communication is known as feedback. Since the beginning of time, we have all experienced feedback on all our actions, as children, students, performers and so on. We need to learn more about feedback as a tool. It is not only the mark at the end of the school year or performance cycle, it should be ongoing as a nutrient in our conditioning for success. There are great programs and tools to employ and use feedback for growth, but when it's only the institutional usage, it tends to be forgotten. It is essential to provide open and honest feedback on just about anything in business, to constantly crawl your workforce, workplace and marketplace to understand where you stand, individually and as a management team. Explore the programs and see what would work in your situation. If you are starting this cold, prepare yourself for the anonymity factor, when the unidentified comments may shock you. Throw out the bottom and top extreme feedback comments and you'll start to understand fully where you are, what you lack and how you can strategically address it for success.

Strength through Conditioning

Athletes are demonstrably strong. They work out to gain mass and endurance, practice good nutrition habits and become mentally fit. Athletes prepare by scouting their opponents, strategically planning for competition and vie for the best to join their teams. The best teams hire specialists, coaches who target the mind, body or soul and bring out the best performances under the most stressful or chaotic situations. That's a formula for success and continued excellence.

What happens to the teams with less resources and means than others? Often, they will be successful to a point. They tend to be more conservative, stretching a budget and getting more out of their resources than others may have to. They will set expectations accordingly and try to advance incrementally year over year. When they win, it's clearly called over achievement. Or, could it be attributed to great leaders on and off the field? From the front office, scouting, marketing and team, all can rise to the top. They may have learned lessons and adjusted often to changing conditions. The term underdog is important to comprehend in sports. The underdog is usually the athlete or team with less expected of them, and when they achieve great success, it shows up as extra preparation, effort, exemplary performance under the toughest conditions.

Is business really that different that sport? As a manager, you need to set expectations based on your personal experience, assigned workforce and workplace environment. Where will you get the support for conditioning your mind, body and soul to succeed in your business? Think of it in whatever terms work, such as the sports mindset reference above. Learn about your company, industry and workforce. What does it take to be good or the best at what you do and what your workforce does? Where do they come from, what is the best course of education, experience and skills training to make this succeed? Even as important a factor will be what he motivation is within anyone who wants to work in your workplace and how you can exploit the best opportunities to grow a world class operation, in any business and any environment.

Who is your conditioning coach? Who do you lean on for continuing education and learning? Who is in your inner circle as a mentor or would you consider on a personal board of directors? These answers to these questions are important as you grow as a manager and as a leader. Who can give you feedback, straightforward conversation and allow you to make better and more confident decisions? Your personal coaching staff will help you to be prepared for the business today and the changes coming tomorrow. Those leaders all have people they lean on and talk to. They all have people and organizations they trust to dispense sound judgment and decision making techniques for managers to share and follow.

HR Certifies Integrity

Management should be organized and authorized. That means there are standards of execution and overall performance that come with the role. You can do well by subscribing to best practices and managing with integrity and honesty. Human Resources is a self-examining community as well as a forward-thinking institution. Managers can earn trust from their workforce when they display soft skills and professional characteristics. HR training is very important to anyone who manages a workforce or oversees the environment where people come to collaborate in a business setting. The HR community take their roles very seriously and the value proposition is they can help the business units to stay compliant and defensible in a conflict. The great organizations that consult and/or train HR professionals, which also includes higher education, take steps to qualify and certify the training and create standards for acceptance and approval.

Take the time to research the various leaders, organizations and consulting companies who have online presence. They offer a lot of valuable information across all the HR disciplines and much of the information is free. Many of them offer discussion or chat forums. These are also good information vaults as you can interact with many of the best thought leaders. You may not always agree with the sentiment or conclusions but will respect the fact that nearly all business situations have historically been acted out and resolved previously and those case studies will help you as you grow in the role. Don't wait until your manager or leader opens a discussion about growth and development, start that research and exploration on your own and be ahead of the curve. Your leadership will recognize your progression. Have a dialogue with your leaders so they know you are willing and committed to achieve and develop as a manager and a leader.

Advocate for HR

As a manager, you want the trust if both your workforce and your leadership. In many companies that are built upon customer service, you also want your clients, customers, vendors, etc. to trust as well. Your acts and communication will be a step towards gaining and fostering trust. Your training for the role may have started with or be based primarily on your background and experience in the business you're working in. Your success as a manager will be based very much on how you learn to implement the soft skills, which are competencies attributed to leading teams, managing people, communicating with skill and grace, etc. If the managing role is new, work on learning about it, following good leaders and practicing new techniques. It will be a curve to overcome and well worth the time and effort to invest. Don't wait to practice once you're in the role, take the time to learn away for the job, on line or with other experienced HR professionals. Prepare yourself for the eventuality of chaos, crisis or confusion and become the voice of reason. Not all decisions are popular and managers must stand by the company decisions, whether they like them or not. A good manager leads the team and protects the company brand.

HR training will allow you a depth of knowledge and a base of information to continually sift through and lean on for decisions. Soft skills are important to eventually master if you want to become a great manager. Fair, balanced and equitable decision-making is a hallmark of HR training and will prove to be the most valuable way for a business to move forward. Solid management will always lift a business as a differentiator. Advocate on behalf of your HR skills, your HR partners or outsourced resources. Make your workforce aware of your support for HR and the expertise and skills that community offers, whether in person or what it has taught you. Your words, actions and overall support will make you confident in your role as a manager.

Talent Acquisition is Core

People are still the most valuable resource in any company. Managing people may be the most difficult and challenging role a manager has. There are so many aspects to respecting and motivating the workforce as individuals, as a team and as integral components to the workflow of business. Managers should use their best intuition, training and/or practices available to ensure the quality of the experience of the workforce. People in your business start started their relationship with your business because of best practices in marketing, recruiting and the talent acquisition process. A few key aspects of recruitment and retention included your commitments to training, diversity, customer service and team building.

Your workforce is a special group of people, no matter what business or industry you're in. Demographics play a big part in collaboration so it's a good practice to include rather than exclude in most situations. Good business culture starts with safe and secure environment and good people. The workforce will be successful if they reflect the business goals, the marketplace and the consumer base for your products or services. Listen to your workforce and give then a forum to open dialogue, recommend change and accept decisions, no matter the resolution.

Communication has been a widely researched and frequent topic in this book and for one more reason, it needs to be reinforced with respect to your workforce. The way you speak or message to your public out in the marketplace and to those prospects looking for work on the outside and in consideration of your company, is important. Those could be the first connections that a candidate for employment will attach themselves to. Are you aware of what messages they received or contact they had previously? Soon, they could be making a heartfelt decision to commit to your company and to you as a manager. Managers need to remember what it was like to search for a job and what the candidate experiences during the process. Whether waiting for a call back to interview or waiting on an offer for a job, the candidate experience is as important as any other process once they are part of the workforce. How you make that first impression says a lot about your professional character. A candidate will always ask, "What's next?

What's Next?

There are many ways and means to get blogs, newsletters, white papers, webinars, presentations, continuing education and other training materials to help inform both managers and aspiring HR professionals. Social media and internet platforms deliver volumes of research solutions and opinion several times daily. You can find many discussion forums and even critical findings via simple query. Take advantage of the immediate resources available as most of them are free with just a submission of your contact information so the contributors know who is consuming their information. Include HR or consulting organizations to follow on line or get email alerts and consider looking at other contributors such as accounting, legal, technology or other industry leaders to follow and interact. They all have real time and relevant business content to share. You can learn quite a bit about best business practices by using the reference power and search capabilities of the mobile and internet platforms.

Managers are important people. They organize, motivate and develop the workforce around them, no matter how small or large a company. These roles are as important to a business as any others. The HR community is a very well-intended, educated and certified collection of dedicated professionals across the spectrum of all things important to workforce and the organization. This is the institution available to many large companies on the inside and still many others as external support vendors. If you cannot afford the partnership, this book should help with HR Insight.

Human Resources has a brand that contains a very important message. They advocate on behalf of companies everywhere. They are educated and certified as professional practitioners of support for protecting company brand and workforce everywhere. They are trained in the sourcing, developing, diversity, performance managing, compensating and ultimately exiting of workforce in your company. Each of these HR disciplines has a specialized industry to support it, consisting of leaders and organizations who continually improve and innovate ways to succeed in business. In the absence of this support, your role as manager may expect that you will step in to one or more of these obligations. Are you ready to deliver what's next in your company?

REFERENCES

Suggested Reference Material:

Linked:HR (#1 Human Resources Group) - https://www.linkedin.com/groups/3761/profile

OD Advocate - https://odadvocate.wordpress.com/free-resources/

Ready to Manage (blog) - http://blog.readytomanage.com/

TradePub (The Professional Research Library) - http://www.tradepub.com/

WordPress - https://la.wordpress.com/tag/organizational-development/

Crucial Conversations - By Kerry Patterson, Joseph Grenny, Ron McMillan, and Al Switzler

Perfect Phrases Books - Books for Managers

The Big Book of HR - By Barbara Mitchell and Cornelia Gamlen (comprehensive HR)

The Everything HR Kit - By John Putzier and David Baker (attracting and retaining great employees)

Every Town is a Sports Town: Business Leadership at ESPN, from the Mailroom to the Boardroom

- By Donald Phillips and George Bodenheimer

A Sampling of Consulting Companies who have Influenced Me:

Aon Hewitt - http://www.aon.com/human-capital-consulting/default.jsp

Center for Creative Leadership - https://www.ccl.org/

CEO Trust - https://ceotrust.org/

Corporate Leadership Council (Gartner) - https://www.cebglobal.com/human-resources.html

Deloitte - http://www2.deloitte.com/us/en.html

Development Dimensions International (DDI) - http://www.ddiworld.com/

Diversity, Inc. - http://www.diversityinc.com/

Electronic Recruiting Exchange (ERE) - http://www.eremedia.com/ere/

Gatti & Associates – http://www.gattihr.com/

Harvard Business Review - https://hbr.org/

Hay Group - http://www.haygroup.com/

Human Capital Institute (HCI) - http://www.hci.org/

Marcum - http://www.marcumllp.com/

Mercer - http://www.mercer.com/

Qualigence International - http://qualigence.com/

Society of Human Resources Management (SHRM) - https://www.shrm.org/

The Aspen Institute - https://www.aspeninstitute.org/

World at Work (The Total Rewards Association) - https://www.worldatwork.org/home/html/home.jsp

Sampling of My Personal Influencers:

John Wooden – Preparation and Teamwork

Michael Bloomberg – Global Responsibility

Annie George – Career Counseling